COMMON GROUND

D0188040

GARY Y. OKIHIRO

Common Ground

*Reimagining
American History*

PRINCETON UNIVERSITY PRESS   PRINCETON AND OXFORD

Copyright ©2001 by Gary Y. Okihiro
Published by Princeton University Press, 41 William Street,
Princeton, New Jersey 08540
In the United Kingdom: Princeton University Press, 3 Market Place,
Woodstock, Oxfordshire OX20 1SY

Library of Congress Cataloging-in-Publication Data

Okihiro, Gary Y., 1945–
Common ground : reimagining American history / Gary Y. Okihiro.
p. cm.
Includes bibliographical references and index.
ISBN 0-691-07006-7—ISBN 0-691-07007-5 (pbk.)
1. United States—History—Philosophy. 2. National characteristics,
American. 3. Minorities—United States—Social conditions.
4. Asian Americans—Social conditions. 5. Group identity—United States.
6. Subjectivity—Social aspects—United States. 7. Binary
principle (Linguistics) 8. Pluralism (Social sciences)—
United States. 9. United States—Ethnic relations. 10. United States—
Social conditions—1980– I. Title.

E175.9.O38 2001
973—dc21   00-049112

This book has been composed in Palatino

The paper used in this publication
meets the minimum requirements of
ANSI/NISO Z39.48-1992 (R1997)
(Permanence of Paper)

www.pup.princeton.edu
Printed in the United States of America

10 9 8 7 6 5 4 3 2 1

To Libs

CONTENTS

ILLUSTRATIONS

I remember the joys of playing cowboys and Indians as a boy. It did not seem strange, at the time, that my friends and I lived in Hawaii on the island of Oahu in a sugar plantation camp with cane fields on one side and a huge sugar mill on the other—it didn't seem incongruous. We would mount our steeds made of old broomstick handles and ride off into the sunset. Of course, we would quarrel over who would be the cowboys, and who the Indians. We patterned ourselves after the Lone Ranger, although playing Tonto, with his quiet ways, his painted face, and his buckskin clothes, had its subversive appeal. "Who was that masked man?", "Hi yo, Silver, away!," and "Kimo sabe!" were expressions we mimicked from the T.V. show. Our role-playing in that make-believe Western came to an end only when our mothers called us to eat our dinners of Spam and rice.

"Playing Indian," historian Philip J. Deloria reminds us, is as American as apple pie or Spam and rice.[1] It might have begun with the Boston Tea Party in 1773 when the Sons of Liberty— white men cross-dressed as Indians—whooped up war cries, boarded tea ships, dumped the cargo into the harbor, and performed in what serves to this day as a theater of the rebellion that defined the national character and subject. The creation of that "American," as opposed to the European colonist in America, was as much a repulsion of the Indian savage as an embrace of the Indian, who exemplified freedom, innocence, and the spirit of the New World. Of course, in my time, playing Indian simultaneously meant playing cowboy. They were two sides of the same coin, like the binary Indian—savage and noble savage—played by white men in red-face at a British-inspired "tea party." (The tea, I should interject, came from Asia.) And cowboys were almost always the "good guys," and Indians, the "bad guys," who invariably lost the wars.

Common Ground is about the creation of the American character and subject. I have conceived this work as an uneasy and troubling companion to general considerations of American history, which, it seems to me, are frequently designed to shape a national identity—the "American"—through a singular narrative of the past. I intend to question the all-too-often easy and smooth flow of that story by asking how the minority subjects, especially Asian Americans, help us to rethink our notions of who "we" are as a people and nation. The core of those ideas of citizenship and history consists of normative assumptions about geographies, race, gender, and sexuality and the binaries that comprise and sustain them. I take up each of those topics in the chapters of this book, and attempt to show that they are inventions of our imaginaries, albeit with real impacts upon our behaviors and lives, and that they are intimate and knowing partners. They form couplings and are inseparable in American history, albeit with peculiar meanings and manifestations, whether visiting them during the late eighteenth, nineteenth, or twentieth centuries.

Geographies are writings upon the earth, like maps that locate and name places and fences that mark boundaries and convert spaces into properties. The attributions of "West" and "East," the principal geographical binary in American history, are my concern in chapter 1. As manly inscriptions upon (womanly) virgin soil, geographies come with correlates, natures such that the West, or the American interior and heartland, is commonly associated with renewal, plenty, homogeneity, stability, union, citizenship, and whiteness; and the East, with the past, poverty, heterogeneity, instability, disunion, alienness, and nonwhiteness. Those geographical binaries I show through a consideration of the minority and Asian American subject to be inventions that are raced, gendered, classed, nationalized, and sexualized and that are false distinctions and mere illusions.

Racializations too are man-made inscriptions, this time upon the human body, and like geographies they form grids that mark the self in opposition to its other. Segregation and spatial separations were attempts to police those creations of difference and preserve the principal racialized binary in America of "white" and "black." Even as West and East come with characters, white and black carry valuations of good and evil, rich and poor, civil and savage, man and woman, citizen and alien, normality and deviance. The Asian American subject, imposed upon that binary, required a revision of categories from white and black to "white" and "nonwhite" that is equally arbitrary and hierarchical. Chapter 2 explores that terrain and discovers a more cluttered territory of racializations than the standard road maps appear to present.

Asians embody the geographies of the East and nonwhiteness, and the gendering that delineates "woman." The Asian body, as argued in chapter 3, reveals that there are within the American imaginary masculine races and feminine races, and normative genders and deviant genders. White manliness in late-nineteenth-century America was made, in part, in the nation's imperial project in Asia and the Pacific and in the conquest by remasculinized white American men of feminized Asian and Pacific peoples, even as white womanliness and the "new" woman were enabled by Asian American men domestics, who performed feminine duties and, like women, were passive and asexual. Those imagined characteristics that accompany the binary of "man" and "woman" are genderings, geographies, and racializations, as the minority and Asian American subjects show, and are performances that script the privileges of man over woman, West over East, white over nonwhite.

White manly heterosexual drives constituted correlates, within nineteenth-century representations, of lesbians and nonwhite women, and of white womanly sexual repressions with gays and nonwhite men. The Asian body, as outlined in chapter 4, is marked by a cluster of natures, including those of geography, race, gender, and sexuality, and by the binaries of the West, whiteness, manliness, heterosexuality, and the citizen—as opposed to the East, nonwhiteness, womanliness, homosexuality or deviant heterosexuality, and the alien. But those invented categories and contrasts, including the binary of "heterosexual" and "homosexual," point to the interconnectedness of the self and the other (they stand in opposition and mutual dependence), and to the fraught and changeable shorelines that at once separate and link supposed poles.

Binaries offer coherence, especially during times of social upheaval. They preserve rule amidst apparent chaos, and stability amidst rapid change, such as during the late eighteenth, nineteenth, and twentieth centuries. Those periods of American history occasioned social reconstitutions of geographies, race, gender, sexuality, and nationality that helped to define and regulate identities, the state, and the social formation. The reconstructions of the late nineteenth century were aided particularly by a science of race, gender, and sexuality, and by laws that restricted immigration even as the nation expanded its borders to America's Far and Wild West and to Asia and the Pacific. Chapter 5 reminds us that, like social categories and their binaries, "American history" itself is a representation that is conditioned by its times and its authors, including this book, which arises from debates over the very nature of America and its people and from my engagement with those contentions.

The "common ground" of this book is neither singular nor exclusive. It conjures the middle ground of the imaginary West and its peoples of common folk and community, of the plain and simple, of common speech and the vernacular. But it also imagines a rich and abundant diversity of landscapes and social relations—geographies, races, genders, sexualities, citizenships—absent unions for members only, binaries of oppositions, valuations of one over the other. In an earlier book, *Margins and Mainstreams: Asians in American History and Culture*, I tried to renarrate American history by taking its binaries and inverting them. Asians did not come to America, I wrote, Americans went to Asia; the mainstream is not the bearers of America's core values, I argued, the margins are.[2] But I have since come to realize that binaries themselves privilege one over the other and thereby constitute hierarchies of difference and inequality.[3] In this work, I reimagine American history by urging that binaries be rejected and be replaced by an open, borderless, and more equitable and just society and nation. We, the people, hold that future in our hands.

In positing the contingent nature of geography, race, gender, and sexuality, I do not mean to discount their spatial or physical realities. Because they are socially constructed, because they are inventions of the mind does not negate their physicalities, their bodily presences, their biologies. The ideas associated with "man" and "woman," for example, are simply that—ideas—but they also plot genetic or somatic markings that map "man" as distinctive from "woman." At the same time, a precise, unwavering dividing line between "man" and "woman" as surveyed by biology is difficult to ascertain and codify (there are intervening gradients and complicating exceptions), and we know that while genetics might determine architectures, impose limitations, and coax inclinations, we also understand that behavior can (re)-shape biology and that biology, like all sciences, is to a degree socially constructed. There are uncertainties and subjectivities even within this science of difference. I am not, however, concerned herein with biology, nor am I denying its possibilities in mapping genetic or bodily differences in the matter of race, gender, or sexuality. Those categories, it seems to me, bear those markings of biology, but they also carry aspects of behavior and psychology that are, assuredly, socially and historically situated, created, and contested.

In composing this version of America's past, I am grateful to Monica McCormick of the University of California Press, who first proposed this book, and to Thomas LeBien of Princeton University Press, who saw this project to its completion. Seminars and audiences at the University of California, Davis, the University of California, San Diego, Macalester College, and the University of Oregon, and American studies scholars in Korea, heard, read, and commented upon versions of several chapters. Comments from my colleagues and friends—Linda Martín Alcoff, Sarah Deutsch, Chris Friday, George Lipsitz, Lisa Lowe, and Clyde A. Milner II—were especially helpful. I am particularly indebted to Peggy Pascoe and her graduate seminar at the University of Oregon for their insightful criticisms of this book's first three chapters, and to members of my 1997 Cornell graduate seminar in Asian American historiography, who tolerated my periodic enthusiasms for this book's subject matters. Sean Sachio Ritch Okihiro gave me his generation's read, and the Cornell undergraduates in my 1998 American history survey class tested several of my theses. All have helped me (re)think my arguments and bring a degree of sobriety to my writing.

And yet, there is a passion here, a rage, a delirium. Over the last several years, I have been in an absolute funk over the persistence of the binaries I herein critique. Like cockroaches they survive, nay thrive, in environments old and new, diminutive and prodigious, noxious and wholesome. They scurry about, those binaries, despite ice ages, urban pollution, and exterminators. The situation can exasperate.

COMMON GROUND

.

CHAPTER 1

West and East

The Wonderful Wizard of Oz is foremost an American fairy tale. The story, briefly, is about how Dorothy, a young Kansas girl, is displaced by a midwestern cyclone, deposited in the land of the Munchkins, and searches for the Wonderful Wizard of Emerald City in Oz, who, she believes, can help her get back to Kansas. On her journey, Dorothy meets and is joined by the Scarecrow, Tin Woodman, and Cowardly Lion, each of whom seeks something, like Dorothy, from the Wonderful Wizard. When they finally meet the Wizard, they discover that he is a fraud, not a wizard at all but a former circus performer from Omaha, a fellow midwesterner. He, nonetheless, shows how each of his supplicants—the Scarecrow, the Tin Woodman, and the Cowardly Lion—already possess what they had sought, and tells how Glinda the Good, the sorceress of the South, reveals to Dorothy that she, too, already has the means by which to return to Kansas—her silver shoes. After clicking her heels, Dorothy and Toto are transported home to Aunt Em and Uncle Henry. "I'm so glad to be at home again!" exclaims a contented Dorothy in the end.

The book was written, according to its author L. Frank Baum, "solely to pleasure children of today." But, published in 1900, it was more than a child's story. It reflected the historical circumstances that swirled around Baum, like the Kansas winds that swept Dorothy and Toto to Munchkin country. Born in central New York in 1856, Baum grew up in a well-to-do home, spent most of his life in Chicago, and moved to Hollywood, where he died in 1919. In writing children's stories, according to his publicist, Baum sought to move away from a European motif and create a distinctively American genre.[1] Kansas provided that most American of places for Baum.

The American heartland surely sets the stage for this saga, along with its virtues of family and home, companionship, sympathy for the underdog, practicality and common sense, and self-reliance. But it is also juxtaposed with the apparent utopia of Oz. Kansas, we are told at the story's beginning, is a flat, desolate place, a "great gray prairie" without a tree or house in sight. The sun bakes the soil dry, burns the grass, and blisters the paint on the house. "When Aunt Em came there to live she was a young, pretty wife," the story goes. "The sun and wind had changed her, too. They had taken the sparkle from her eyes and left them a sober gray; they had taken the red from her cheeks and lips, and they were gray also. She was thin and gaunt, and never smiled, now." Uncle Henry, like Aunt Em, "never laughed," and he worked hard from morning till night and rarely spoke.[2]

In contrast, Oz was filled with bright sunshine and was "a country of marvelous beauty." Instead of the treeless gray of Kansas, there were "lovely patches of green sward all about, with stately trees bearing rich and luscious fruits. Banks of gorgeous flowers were on every hand, and birds with rare and brilliant plummage sang and fluttered in the trees and bushes. A little way off was a small brook, rushing and sparkling along between green banks. . . ." That stark contrast between Kansas and Oz was just one of several dualisms within Baum's story. Oz itself was divided into north and south, east and west, each with their respective witches. His contemporaries no doubt recognized Baum's contrasts and dualisms. Aunt Em and Uncle Henry's condition surely resonated with the plight of the midwestern farmer who not only faced the ravages of nature but also the bondage of eastern capital. Baum was a supporter of the Democratic party's 1896 standard bearer, William Jennings Bryan, who trumpeted the call for the "free coinage of silver" (recollect the color of Dorothy's magical shoes) as beneficial to farmers and the working class, and who opposed the capitalists' "cross of gold." The Tin Woodman had once been a hardworking human being, but, by the very necessity of labor (each swing of his axe had chopped off a part of his body), Eastern witchcraft, or the industrial machine, had transformed his body into metal (smiths had

Fig. 1. *American Gothic,* by Grant Wood (1930).

"Dorothy lived in the midst of the great Kansas prairies, with Uncle Henry, who was a farmer, and Aunt Em, who was the farmer's wife. Their house was small. . . . [Aunt Em] was thin and gaunt, and never smiled now. . . . Uncle Henry never laughed. He worked hard from morning till night and did not know what joy was." Quotation from Michael Patrick Hearn (ed.), *The Annotated Wizard of Oz* (New York: Clarkson N. Potter, 1973). *American Gothic* (oil on beaverboard, 74.3 × 62.4 cm) courtesy of The Art Institute of Chicago, Friends of American Art Collection, and VAGA, New York, NY, 1930.934. All rights reserved.

replaced his bodily parts with tin). The urban factory of the East encounters the agrarian ideal of the West.[3]

The contrasts were more apparent than real. It was like the discoveries made by Dorothy, the Scarecrow, the Tin Woodman, and the Cowardly Lion: what seemed real was illusion, and what they had set out to find they already possessed. Dorothy wears

the shoes that take her home, the Scarecrow exhibits much common sense, the Tin Woodman weeps after stepping on a beetle,
and the Cowardly Lion learns that fear is normal. What appears
absent is really present. Similarly, the plainness and gray of Kansas only seemed at odds with the greenness and light of Oz; they
also bore like features. The cornfields, peach trees, crows, beetles,
wildcats, storks, and field mice of Kansas populate the landscape
of Oz, and both places are rural and filled with farmers and
woodsmen. And despite the misery of Kansas, Dorothy comes
to the conclusion after her wonderful mystical journey that
"there is no place like home." "No matter how dreary and gray
our homes are," Dorothy explains to the Scarecrow, "we people
of flesh and blood would rather live there than in any other
country, be it ever so beautiful." The utopian attractions and possibilities of Oz were always present in Kansas and the American
heartland.[4]

Two of the most persistent and pervasive myths of America's
past are the idea of the West and the idea of the West as the nation's frontier. America's history, indeed its uniqueness and national identity, is rooted within that imaginary space, the un-
turned sod, the "virgin land" of the portable frontier that moved
from the Atlantic seaboard to the Alleghenies, to the Mississippi,
the Great Plains, the Rockies, and California's golden shore, and
to the Pacific and Asia. According to the myth, that "westering"—imagining and mapping, expanding and conquering, set-
tling and building—tamed a howling wilderness, brought light
to darkness, and molded a "new man." No longer a European,
he was an American, as original and distinctive as the environment that shaped him.

In the West, along the frontier or the divide between civilization and barbarism, "the wilderness masters the colonist" wrote
historian Frederick Jackson Turner, giving him "coarseness and
strength combined with acuteness and inventiveness," a "practi-
cal, inventive turn of mind," a "dominant individualism," and a
"buoyancy and exuberance which comes with freedom." These
were among the core American virtues that were distilled within
the crucible of the frontier.[5] A young, assistant professor at the

University of Wisconsin at the time, Turner outlined his frontier hypothesis in a paper presented at the 1893 meeting of the American Historical Association in Chicago, coinciding with that city's hosting of the 1893 World's Fair. The timing and place of those events were propitious. The temper of the times—as Turner had written earlier in an observation that applies equally to historians and storytellers—conditions the choice of historical subject matters and their interpretations. "Each age," he had perceptively declared, "tries to form its own conception of the past. Each age writes the history of the past anew with reference to conditions uppermost in its own time."[6]

The late nineteenth century, as is evident in *The Wonderful Wizard of Oz*, saw the rise of agrarian populism—the revolt of western farmers against the perceived tyranny of eastern capital that was fueled by class as well as by regional antagonisms and interests. Chicago's selection over cities of the eastern establishment as the site for the 1893 World's Fair was significant, along with its theme—a celebration of the four-hundredth anniversary of Columbus's "discovery" of the Americas. And though by 1893 the course of empire, with its frontiers to America's south in Cuba and Puerto Rico and to its west in the Philippines and Hawaii, had yet to be fully run, that destiny of European peoples had long been envisioned, at least since the Republic's founding and, in truth, since Columbus's expedition to India and the regions beyond.

Turner's immediate concern was the report of the 1890 U.S. Census, which declared that because of settlement, "there can hardly be said to be a frontier line." "The frontier has gone," in Turner's words, "and with its going has closed the first period of American history." The frontier's closing, however, meant more than the end of an epoch; it foreshadowed a denial of access to the generative lands that gave Americans their rugged individualism, their unrestrained exuberance, their sinewy toughness. "This, then, is the real situation: a people composed of heterogeneous materials, with diverse and conflicting ideals and social interests, having passed from the task of filling up the vacant spaces of the continent, is now thrown back upon itself, and is seeking an equilibrium," explained Turner in an 1896 essay. "The diverse elements are being fused into national unity. The forces of reorganization are turbulent and the nation seems like a witches' kettle."[7]

An aspect of that "witches' kettle" were the diverse and unprecedented masses of immigrants who were streaming to America's eastern shores during the late nineteenth century. Unlike America's traditional immigrants, the 25 million who migrated to the United States between 1865 and 1915 did not come from Britain, Ireland, or northern Europe alone, but also from Italy, Greece, Poland, Russia, China, Japan, Korea, India, and the Philippines, and they totaled more than four times the number of those who had arrived during the previous fifty years. They flocked to the Northeast and West, where factories, in cities and fields, were humming, and where barons of industry and agriculture were monopolizing chunks of land, natural resources, and capital, and accumulating great wealth.

Ethnic and class conflicts were commonplace. In 1886 Chicago, in America's heartland, police killed four strikers, and the next day a bomb killed seven officers and injured sixty-seven people. The Haymarket Square bombing came to symbolize, for many Americans, the imagined threat posed by southern and eastern Europeans, immigrants, radicals, and anarchists. "These people," a Chicago newspaper reported of the Haymarket strikers, "are not American, but the very scum and offal of Europe." Americans were not solely concerned with Europe's "rubbish." In 1882, four years before Haymarket, Congress passed the Chinese Exclusion Act because, in the words of the Act, "the coming of Chinese laborers to this country endangers the good order of certain localities within the territory thereof." In 1894, the American Protective Association, a nativist group committed to stopping the immigrant tide, reportedly had a membership of 500,000, drawn from the Northeast and also from the Midwest.[8] "Thrown back upon itself," the nation—a "witches' kettle"— steamed and boiled and bubbled.

In the glare of these new social realities at the close of the nineteenth century, Turner's frontier hypothesis is forward-looking but also nostalgic, drawing upon a myth expressed at least a hundred years earlier during the late eighteenth century. The agrarian tradition, as described by literary scholar Henry Nash Smith, was a self-image that defined what Americans thought about themselves and their past, present, and future. The tradition was inward-looking, distinctly not European, and captured a hankering for and a faith in an inland empire of near-infinite expanse and untapped wealth that exuded from the fecund and blessed land. That species of American nationalism, wrote Smith, was expressed even before America's independence and later in countless "rhapsodies on the West" by visionaries who saw the American interior "as a new and enchanting region of inexpressible beauty and fertility," of stately forests and rich meadows on which roamed vast herds of animals and where a thousand rivers flowed into the mighty Mississippi. And although expansive, the agrarian tradition, noted Smith, "made it difficult for Americans to think of themselves as members of a world community because it has affirmed that the destiny of this country leads her away from Europe toward the agricultural interior of the continent."[9]

Those romantic ideas of the trans-Appalachian West had precedents one hundred years earlier at the close of the eighteenth century, despite indications of a contrary, nonagrarian future evidenced in the rise of British industrialism and America's first modern factory—a spinning mill erected in Pawtucket, Rhode Island, in 1790. And like its 1890s version, the agrarian tradition of the 1790s helped galvanize a national identity that in the late eighteenth century contributed to the fall of the Federalists and the rise of the Republicans and Jeffersonian democracy in the election of 1800. The Federalists, who favored government by a powerful elite over a passive citizenry, were tied to Europe, hereditary rule, and the Old World by their opponents, the Republicans, who united disparate groups and classes around the notions of popular sovereignty and democracy that they claimed as distinctively American and native to the New World.[10] It is not surprising, thus, that the singular hero of Jeffersonian democracy was the intrepid, independent pioneer and farmer who fled Europe, cleared America's forests, settled, cultivated an abundance, and brought forth a new man and nation. And the Republican geographical distinctions of Old World and New World, Europe and America, East and West, paralleled the agrarian tradition's domestic orientations of old and new, the Atlantic seaboard and the interior, East and West, and its associations of rebirth, plenitude, and the American identity with the West.

Jefferson's purchase of Louisiana from France in 1803, doubling the nation's size and extending its western frontier, was in one sense an affirmation of the agrarian ideal. According to Henry Nash Smith, Jefferson was "the intellectual father of the American advance to the Pacific."[11] He collected information on Louisiana from the British, Spanish, and French when he served as an American diplomat in Paris from 1784 to 1789, and as President he dispatched Meriwether Lewis and William Clark in 1803 to find a route to the Pacific "for the purposes of commerce."[12] Although impractical at the time as an economic scheme, Lewis and Clark's expedition, wrote Smith, "lay on the level of imagination; it was drama, it was the enactment of a myth that embodied the future. It gave tangible substance to what had been merely an idea, and established the image of a highway across the continent so firmly in the minds of Americans that repeated failures could not shake it." And when Lewis and Clark camped on the shore of the Pacific in 1805, Smith observed, "They reactivated the oldest of all ideas associated with America—that of a passage to India."[13]

The agrarian tradition found the American identity neither in Europe nor along the nation's teeming eastern seaboard, but within its "vacant" interior called its "heartland." There, among the forests and plains seemingly devoid of humanity (wherein American Indians were included among the wilderness requiring domestication) and diversity, British, Irish, and northern Europeans blended into a distinctive, yet homogeneous, racial and cultural stock—the American. "What then is the American, this new man?" asked French immigrant and American farmer J. Hector St. John de Crèvecoeur in 1782. "*He* is an American, who leaving behind him all his ancient prejudices and manners, receives new ones from the new mode of life he has embraced, the new government he obeys, and the new rank he holds. He becomes an American by being received in the broad lap of our great *Alma Mater*. Here individuals of all nations are melted into a new race of men."[14] Eighty years later in an essay titled "Walking," Henry David Thoreau wrote of westward migration as symbolic of America's near-limitless reach. "I must walk toward Oregon, and not toward Europe," Thoreau stated, because "the future, with a spirit of enterprise and adventure" awaited the westward walker, because in the West could be found "an area of equal extent with that occupied by the bulk of our States, so fertile and so rich and varied in its productions, and at the same time so habitable by the European," because the West's mountain air "feeds the spirit and inspires," allowing men to grow "to greater perfection intellectually as well as physically."[15]

The belief that the West held transformative powers in shaping and reshaping people provided the rationale for Charles Loring Brace and his New York Children's Aid Society to combat juvenile delinquency by sending wayward youth and "orphans" to the West in the 1850s. Removed from the degenerative influences and temptations of city life, Brace contended, and placed within the virtuous environs of nature and the farm, children who had been deformed and made ill by the unnatural contrivances of the city could be remade and restored to social health. By 1910, the society had sent over 110,000 children.[16] The West, a region of the country but also an idea summoned in the simple yet significant term "the heartland," came to embody the values and virtues of the nation.

By an act of Congress in 1785, the lands west of the Appalachians were surveyed, divided into rectangular grids, and sold in disregard of the natural contours of the land, its diverse environments, and the peoples who lived and moved across its expanses. This Northwest Territory, so named by Congress two years later, eventually came to occupy not only the geographical center of the nation but also its common ground, according to many observers. "To the frontier came an all-American society," wrote a native midwesterner. Yankees and southerners brought their different cultures and speech with them, and in the melting pot of the Midwest these distinctions vanished. "In time the Southern drawl and the Yankee twang blended into what has been called the 'general American speech,' and the heartland towns had a vigorous and friendly character of their own," he explained. Those midwesterners, like the land that shaped them, were largely homogeneous, the writer continued. "The land rolls on unchanged; farms, towns and cities repeat the same tempo and impression; people use the same idiom and intonation; they share common attitudes and instincts. This entire region has a common history."[17]

The heartland's location in the middle of the country is more than a geographic phenomenon; it is metaphorical. It is all American, because it is the sum and average of the nation. Midwesterners, according to a historian, know that they are the heart of the continent, and they believe that "the South is backward, the West is a place of extremes, and that the East, although culturally advanced, is effete in character; therefore, all are to be pitied— only midwesterners are true Americans."[18] The poet Dave Etter offers a humorous rendition of those self-proclaimed virtues of centrality and typicality in his poem, "Henry Lichenwalner: Living in the Middle."

> Here in Alliance, Illinois,
> I'm living in the middle,
> standing on the Courthouse lawn
> in the middle of town,
> in the middle of my life,
> a self-confessed middlebrow,
> a member of the middle class,
> and of course Middle Western,
> the middle, you see, the middle,
> believing in the middle way,
> standing here at midday
> in the middle of the year,
> breathing the farm-fragrant air
> of Sunflower County,

in the true-blue middle
of middle America,
in the middle of my dreams.[19]

Of all the nation's regions, a foundational textbook on regionalism declared, "the Middle States may be characterized as the most American of them all. This is not to say that there will not be found in each of the other regions special character traits easily identified as extremely 'American' but that this region combines a larger number than any other region and therefore approximates the first place in any picture of the nation to be envisaged through its major regions." The Midwest, the text's authors explained, epitomizes the two "great motivations" of the nation—migration and westward expansion. It is the ground where Europeans became Americans. "Here were symbol and reality of rivers and forests, of land and prairies, of plain people and democratic patterns, symbols of the American dream. In the quality and number of its people, the nature and number of its occupations, its small industries and great agriculture, in the best examples of balanced industry and agriculture, are typified the heart of America and the backbone of its national framework. And here are American manners and morals, folkways and customs, religion and politics."[20]

The historian Carl L. Becker summarized some of the salient notions of America's heartland in his essay in praise of Kansas written in 1910 when he was a professor at the University of Kansas. The people of Kansas, he maintained, had shaped a community on "the frontier of human endeavor" based upon "an identity of race, custom, habits, needs; a consensus of opinion in respect to morals and politics. . . . Its people are principally American born, descended from settlers who came mainly from the middle west. It is an agricultural state, and the conditions of life are, or have been until recently, much the same for all." There were no millionaires or paupers, mansions or hovels. Its people formed a single class. Kansans, Becker noted, were united on the basis of an "identity of race and uniformity of custom," and from their perception of themselves as unique and different from others. "The Kansas spirit," he proposed, "is the American spirit double distilled. It is a new grafted product of American individualism, American idealism, American intolerance. Kansas is America in microcosm. . . . Within its borders, Americanism, pure and undefiled, has a new lease of life. It is the mission of this self-selected people to see to it that it does not perish from off the earth."[21]

Middle America—all America, real America—was shaped thus by the frontier and its workings that produced the region's people and their character. These were singular, uniform, constant. They were revealed in the people's racial makeup, in their beliefs, in their practices. Bedrock American values thrived there, in middle America, in agrarian America, where Americanism, "pure and undefiled," found a new lease on life. Neither America's East and West coasts, nor its continental borders north and south, could, like Oz's Wonderful Wizard, conjure a magic equal to that of the Midwest. In truth and by contrast, the nation's exterior rim, as viewed from the heartland, recall a messier, more contentious, and even fatal ground.

But all is not well in the heartland. In its differentiation of Americans from those who were not Americans, the agrarian tradition not only promoted nationalism, a legitimate and perhaps necessary precondition for a nation-state, but also stoked a sense of superiority and isolationism. American exceptionalism, as historian Ian Tyrrell has pointed out, or the idea that the United States was unique, separate from Europe and the rest of the world, and an example for other nations to emulate, formed the basis of a resilient nationalist history. Although important, wrote Tyrrell, the nation-state and nationalism are not the totality of history, but they loom large on history's canvas because of "the historian's common-sense observation of the contemporary world" and "the way historical knowledge has been produced." Historical records have been collected, arranged, and deposited in boxes and archives by the state and nation, and they thus condition and encourage certain historical narratives of that state and nation while discouraging others. Historians must break out of those figurative, literal, and confining discourses, exhorted

Tyrrell, by contextualizing national histories within their international or global frames. That project, he contended, does not require a slighting of national histories, but does offer a simultaneous and equal consideration of the local, national, and transnational.[22] In addition to historical parochialism, American exceptionalism is simultaneously a claim to difference or uniqueness and a move that centers and elevates some Americans while marginalizing and denigrating others.[23]

The agrarian tradition, then, simultaneously advanced nationalism and sectionalism, differentiating the New World from the Old, the West from the East, the interior from the coasts. The oceans and their shores, according to this tradition, formed protective moats and embankments that allowed the American variety to germinate and grow, shielding it from foreign tides and blights. But there was a countervailing narrative, Henry Nash Smith informs us, a maritime tradition that extended outward, connecting Americans to their European forebears and original stock.[24] Although apparently at odds one with the other, the maritime tradition in fact complemented the agrarian tradition insofar as America's peoples, as a racialized group, and their institutions and culture all derived from Western European antecedents. The American, whether descending from agrarian or maritime pasts, is essentially European according to these narratives of nation.

A version, perhaps dominant, of the maritime tradition holds that America is the western terminus of an Atlantic civilization comprised of European "cultural hearths" and their trans-Atlantic diasporas and transplantations. Columbus's first landing in 1492 was the start of that Atlantic civilization. From its shores and points of view, Europe was the center, the original, the authenticating source from which flowed peoples, cultures, and institutions. Herbert Baxter Adams, one of Frederick Jackson Turner's professors at Johns Hopkins University, was an influential advocate of the "germ theory" that held that all American institutions derived from medieval Germany and spread with European migrants to the New World. Indeed, Turner's frontier hypothesis turned on its head his mentor's germ theory by

reversing the origin and direction of American identity and institutions; according to Turner, these arose in the American interior
and spread to the coast and thence from the New World to the
Old.[25] Turner's version of the agrarian tradition simply privi-
leged the American side of a European story.

Thomas Jefferson, a man of the soil and an American centrist,
also understood that Americans were an Atlantic and European
people. A true nationalist, he called that relationship the "American system," which envisioned a cord of republican kinship,
achieved through eighteenth- and nineteenth-century revolu-
tions, tying together the nations bordering the north Atlantic
while also setting them apart from the despotisms of central and
eastern Europe. About a hundred years later, Henry Adams
named that transatlantic correspondence the "Atlantic system,"
binding the north Atlantic nations in a "community of interest."
And Forrest Davis, writing on the eve of America's entry into
World War II, argued that the Atlantic system was "old, rational,
and pragmatic," that its roots ran "deep and strong into the
American tradition," and that it had emerged from "strategic
and political realities."[26] More recent studies of Atlantic civilization, like their forebears, reflect the light of contemporary con-
cerns and perspectives in more balanced treatments for both
sides of the Atlantic, greater stresses on the differences as well
as commonalities within the Atlantic community, an acknowleg-
ment that Atlantic civilization's development was built in large
part upon Africa and Latin America's underdevelopment, and in
complex figurations of the Atlantic community as both North
and South, white and black, and bi- and multilateral between
and among Europe, the Americas, and Africa.[27]

The maritime tradition, thus, has the salutary effect of placing
the United States within a more global orbit of Atlantic civilization and asks how Africans and America's indigenous peoples
were drawn into European civilization. And unlike the agrarian
tradition, it now proposes a history transcendent of nation that
has neither national boundaries nor the binaries of Old and New
World and white and black. The black Atlantic, the cultural critic
Paul Gilroy proposes, transgresses the categories of nation, race,

and ethnicity and is emphatically and mutably mixed and hybrid.[28] But like its land-based counterpart, the maritime tradition is incomplete. Slighted are the lands north and south of the United States, the native peoples of the Americas whose histories long preceded the advent of Europe's Atlantic civilization, and Asians who like Africans were transported to labor in the Americas by Europeans and thereby added complexity to the multicultural black Atlantic. And the Atlantic world, however inclusive, still centers Europe and the expansion of its peoples and their deeds upon indigenous Africa and the Americas wherein whites act upon nonwhites.

The Asian American subject, pushed to the foreground of American history, helps us to rethink both the agrarian and maritime traditions. It reminds us that the United States and the Americas are surely elements of the Atlantic world or the black Atlantic, but also are parts of a Pacific world that, like its Atlantic correlate, was a system of flows of capital, labor, and culture that produced transnational and hybrid identities as well as their counterclaims for homogeneity, nationalism, and racial purity. In that sense, the United States is an island surrounded by lands north and south, but also oceans east and west. And as an island, in contrast to the imagined insularity of the agrarian tradition, the United States must be viewed not only as a center with its own integrity but also as a periphery and fluid space of movements and engagements that resist closure and inevitable outcomes. Further, the Midwest and the United States as a whole were never wholly exceptional, homogeneous, or isolated from other regions of the country or the world. The nation's interiors were bound to its coasts and borders, which in turn were bound to the world beyond. The history of Asians in America points out that U.S. history and the American identity are local, national, and transnational in scope, are complex and heterogeneous, and are both inward- and outward-looking, as advanced by both the agrarian and maritime traditions.[29]

In truth, as figured in Atlantic civilization, America's very "discovery" resulted from a transnational project—Europe's ancient and persistent search for a passage to Asia. As noted by

Christopher Columbus in his ship's daily log, his expedition's purpose was to go "to the regions of India, to see the Princes there and the peoples and the lands, and to learn of their disposition, and of everything, and the measures which could be taken for their conversion to our Holy Faith."[30] Columbus, we know, was not the first European who sought the goods and wealth of Asia, but followed a long line of invaders, traders, and dreamers that might have begun with the ancient Greeks of the fifth or fourth century B.C.E.[31]

Asia, according to cultural theorists Edward W. Said and Mary B. Campbell, was Europe's other.[32] Asia was a source of Europe's civilizations and languages, the site of its oldest and richest colonies, and its political and cultural contestant. Orientalism, writes Said, was a "Western style for dominating, restructuring, and having authority over" Asia. Within its lexicon, Asians were inferior to and deformations of Europeans, whose purpose was to stir an inert people, give them form, and bestow upon them an identity. Those gendered representations, wherein Europeans are rendered as men and Asians as women, justified Europe's colonization of Asia by which European men aroused, penetrated, and domesticated the passive, dark, and vacuous "Eastern bride," according to Said.[33]

Orientalism, as Said and the historian Ronald Takaki have pointedly argued, is not a mere discourse of representations, but also supports Europe's and America's masculine thrust toward a feminized Asia—their invasion, conquest, and colonization of Asia.[34] Like Europe's trans-Atlantic diasporas, America's westward march across the frontiers and expanses deemed central to the American epic by the agrarian tradition was, from the Asian American standpoint, an extension of Europe's pursuit after "fabulous" Asia. Not merely inward-bound, the frontier's prairie schooners and wagon trains were like ships that had originated in Europe, docked on the East Coast of the United States, and continued on into the interior and to the West Coast, but also sailed on to Hawaii and Asia.

Jefferson's quest for an overland passage to India might have lain in the realm of imagination, but America's Asian destiny was already a seaborne reality and well under way. Soon after the Republic's founding, on George Washington's birthday in 1784, the *Empress of China* sailed from New York City's harbor, bound for Asia. A "Great Number of Inhabetants," wrote the ship's captain John Green in his log, "Salluted us by giveing Three Cheers," as the *Empress*, with its cargo bay filled with New England ginseng, slipped from its mooring and sailed toward the open sea. The *Empress of China*, "fitted out partly at the expense of Robert Morris, merchant prince and 'financier of the American Revolution,' sailed from New York to Canton, carrying the American flag into the midst of the Dutch and British pennants that fluttered in the breezes of Chinese waters," historian Charles A. Beard wrote. "Before the Fathers completed the framing of the Constitution, at least nine voyages had been made to the Far East by enterprising Yankees." In the year of Washington's inauguration, ten ships from Salem, Massachusetts, sailed the waters of the Indian ocean, and on the date of his retirement to Mount Vernon, in 1797, the *Betsy* returned from China with a cargo that netted $120,000 in profits. In the decade of the 1830s, American trade with China amounted to nearly $75 million, a sum greater than the total debt of the American Revolution, and America's textile factories saw Asia's fecund shores as markets that would keep "their wheels whirling and coffers full."[35]

Jefferson's successors, in particular Missouri's Thomas Hart Benton, championed the cause of western expansion. As senator and congressman during the mid-nineteenth century, Benton articulated and advanced his dream of an American empire built upon trade with Asia. Benton, like many midwesterners, connected America's East Coast with Europe, referring to it as "the English seaboard," where the American spirit, he believed, was stifled by Old World traditions, and instead saw the nation's future in the West, where freedom and greatness could be achieved. Asia was a key to that development for Benton, who contended that all of the great European empires were built upon their access to and monopoly of the Asian trade. America's Pacific destiny, declared Benton, would free the nation from European dependence and inferiority, and complete the journey that

Columbus had begun. "The trade of the Pacific Ocean, of the western coast of North America, and of Eastern Asia," he predicted, "will all take its track; and not only for ourselves, but for posterity. That trade of India which has been shifting its channels from the time of the Phoenicians to the present, is destined to shift once more, and to realize the grand idea of Columbus. The American road to India will also become the European track to that region."[36]

But the course of empire had to be run one race at a time. Even the prophetic Benton could not at first envision America's expansion from sea to shining sea, and instead believed that North America's western lands would comprise a separate nation intermediate between the United States and Asia. His son-in-law, John Charles Fremont, however, played a prominent role in the mapping of the West, the promotion of its American settlement, and the conquest of California. America's invasion and defeat of Mexico and its absorption of Mexico's northern territories in 1848 achieved the first phase of the Republic's (and Europe's) "manifest destiny"; and like Spain's Vasco de Balboa, who traversed the Panamanian isthmus in 1513 and gazed across the Pacific, some of America's leaders viewed a Pacific crossing to the wealth of Asia as the next phase in national expansion. Benton's scheme for American greatness coalesced both the maritime and agrarian traditions in that Asia's products carried on ships would, Benton predicted, land at the nation's western terminus and, during their transcontinental journey to the Northeast, would stimulate the growth of farms, cities, and manufactures within America's interior. "An American road to India through the heart of our country," he proposed, "will revive upon its line all the wonders of which we have read—and eclipse them. The western wilderness, from the Pacific to the Mississippi, will start into life under its touch."[37]

For Asians touched by European peoples, trade, conquest and colonization, and migration commonly followed contact.[38] Some of the first Asian settlers in the Americas came by way of Europe's Asia. Ferdinand Magellan's expedition, from 1519 to 1522, rounded South America's horn, sailed into the Pacific, landed in the Philippines, and claimed the islands for Spain. Beginning in 1565, Spanish ships sailed between Manila and Acapulco, entrepôts of the Spanish empire, in the galleon trade that exchanged Mexico's silver for Asia's spices, silks, porcelain, and furniture and transported them to the Americas and thence to Europe. On board those galleons were impressed and hired sailors, Filipinos and Chinese, some of whom had jumped ship in Acapulco and found their way to Mexico City and, as early as the 1760s, to the bayous of Louisiana, another of Spain's colonies. In the swamps near New Orleans, these Filipino "Manilamen" founded the oldest, continuous Asian communities in North America.[39]

Asian Indians, with anglicized names like James Dunn, John Ballay, Joseph Green, George Jimor, and Thomas Robinson, arrived on America's East Coast in Boston and Philadelphia on board British and American trade vessels during the 1780s and 1790s. Some served their indentures; others were sold and bought as slaves. Historian Joan Jensen speculates that those men, when freed, probably married African American women and became members of the local African American communities. A petition filed "about the 1790's" and contained in the records of the Pennsylvania Abolition Society tells the story of James Dunn, an Asian Indian who had been indentured by his parents to an English sailor when he was eight years old. Passed on from owner to owner, Dunn arrived in the American South, where he tried to regain his freedom, believing that he had served the period of his indenture. His owners, however, treated him as a slave, and the Abolition Society's papers do not indicate whether Dunn ever obtained his freedom.[40] The 1855 New York State census found other Asians who had come to America by way of the Asian trade— Chinese men together with their families, many comprised of Irish women and their biracial offspring, who had been living and working in New York City since the 1820s.[41]

Indeed, America's ports fostered a wide diversity of peoples and cultures. On the Atlantic, the crew of the *Pallas*, according to a witness, consisted of "Chinese, Malays, Japanese and Moors, and a few Europeans," when it docked in Baltimore in 1785. On the Pacific, John Meares of the British East India Company sailed from south China in 1788 with a crew of Chinese shipbuilders, carpenters, metal workers, and sailors. The expedition built a fur-trading and ship-building settlement on Vancouver Island.[42] Lesing Newman and John Islee, Chinese residents of New York City, were sailors based in that port. Newman was a naturalized U.S. citizen bound for Liverpool, England, in 1835, while Islee sailed to Liverpool in 1847. That same year, China-born Ben Sanchez left New York's harbor for Havana. An 1856 *New York Times* article estimated that there were 150 Chinese, most of whom were sailors, living in lower Manhattan.[43]

Demographic and economic changes marked the first half of the nineteenth century in America. About the turn of the century, the nation was essentially rural and agrarian, with modest manufacturing and international trade concentrated in the Northeast. But most Americans were farmers, and their economy and outlook were primarily local. Fifty years later, America had gone through an industrial revolution with its resultant rise in population and workforce, the growth of cities and urban centers of manufacturing and trade, transportation innovations, immigration, and a translocal, national integration. And although most Americans still depended upon agriculture for their economic well-being, the context of that activity had expanded from local to national and international market economies.

The nation's edges, primarily the industrial centers of New York City, Boston, and Philadelphia, led the way and exemplified many of those changes. But even its interior, contrary to the homogeneity assumed by the agrarian tradition and heartland boosters, reflected those national trends. Immigration was a significant cause for the dramatic rise in American population, from a mere 4 million in 1790 to 17 million in 1840. Immigrants totaled nearly half of New York City's population by the 1850s, but they also outnumbered native-born Americans in western cities such as St. Louis, Chicago, and Milwaukee.[44] About the turn of the century, social reformer Jane Addams observed that Chicago's immigrants had laid "the simple and inevitable foundations of an international order" through the cosmopolitan "intermingling of the nations," and African American migrants from the South had formed vibrant communities in that Midwest metropolis.[45] Besides those economic and demographic changes, linguists note the falsity of "general American" English, and instead cite the rich language variations that flourish throughout the Midwest.[46] Those diversities in the heartland, although self-evident and abundant, were easily missed by nationalist myths.

Rather, immigrants and the coast cities to which they seemed to flock constituted an opposition to the supposed homogeneity and tranquility of the interior, and they comprised strange, foreign, and even threatening presences among certain elements of the American imagination of the late nineteenth century. Stirred by the apparent decline of the agrarian ideal and by the intrusion of the noisy machine into America's pristine garden, critics of the new immigration, industrialism, and expansionism lamented the nation's apparent turn to materialism, greed, and barbarism. Editor and poet Thomas Bailey Aldrich, an easterner and a parochialist, warned of America's "Unguarded Gates":

> Wide open and unguarded stand our gates,
> And through them presses a wild motley throng—
> Men from the Volga and the Tartar steppes,
> Featureless figures from the Hoang-Ho,
> Malayan, Scythian, Teuton, Kelt, and Slav,
> Flying the Old World's poverty and scorn;
> These bringing with them unknown gods and rites,
> Those, tiger passions, here to stretch their claws.
> In street and alley what strange tongues are loud,
> Accents of menace alien to our air,
> Voices that once the Tower of Babel knew!
> O Liberty, white Goddess! is it well
> To leave the gates unguarded? On thy breast
> Fold Sorrow's children, soothe the hurts of fate,
> Lift the down-trodden, but with hand of steel
> Stay those who to thy sacred portals come
> To waste the gifts of freedom. Have a care
> Lest from thy brow the clustered stars be torn
> And trampled in the dust. For so of old

The thronging Goth and Vandal trampled Rome,
And where the temples of the Caesars stood
The lean wolf unmolested made her lair.[47]

In a letter dated May 14, 1892, Aldrich confessed: "I went home
and wrote a misanthropic poem called 'Unguarded Gates' . . . in
which I mildly protest against America becoming the cesspool
of Europe. I'm much too late, however," he lamented. "I looked
in on an anarchist meeting the other night . . . and heard such
things spoken by our 'feller citizens' as made my cheek burn. . . .
I believe in America for the Americans; I believe in the widest
freedom and the narrowest license, and I hold that jail-birds, pro-
fessional murderers, amateur lepers . . . and human gorillas generally should be closely questioned at our Gates." Aldrich closed
with his endorsement of Rudyard Kipling's acid observation that
New York City had become "a despotism of the alien, by the
alien, for the alien, tempered with occasional insurrections of
decent folk!"[48]

To some, the immigrant conjured the specter of urban unrest,
class conflict, and poverty. In 1880 Boston, according to an
alarmed observer, three-fifths of the population were foreign
born, and in the mid-1880s there were 555 strikes.[49] Chicago's
Haymarket bloodshed of 1886, called "the work of a lot of pathological Germans and Poles" by the Harvard philosopher William
James, was just one of several major labor clashes in the late nineteenth century. Perhaps most influential was the Pullman strike
of 1894 that affected thousands of railroad workers in twenty-
seven states and territories and paralyzed transportation from
Chicago to the West Coast. Over the objections of Illinois's governor, President Grover Cleveland ordered 2,000 federal troops in
the Chicago area to arrest the strike's leaders, including Eugene
V. Debs, president of the American Railway Union, and to en-
force a court injunction forbidding the strike.

Just as immigrants were linked to class conflict, so were they
paired with poverty. "In the poorest quarters of many great
American cities and industrial communities one is struck by a
most peculiar fact—the poor are almost entirely foreign born,"

declared Robert Hunter, a social worker, in his classic 1904 text, *Poverty*. The alien poor, according to Hunter, formed "colonies, foreign in language, customs, habits, and institutions" and were distinguished from "American groups" by ethnicity and race. In New York City, there were "colonies" of Irish, Jews, Italians, Russians, Poles, Greeks, Syrians, Chinese, and African Americans. "The rich and well-to-do are mostly Americans; the poor are mostly foreign, drawn from among the miserable of every nation," Hunter wrote. "To live in one of these foreign communities is actually to live on foreign soil. The thoughts, feelings, and traditions which belong to the mental life of the colony are often entirely alien to an American." Although they were living in America, he argued, they were not of America. Besides being mired in poverty, poor immigrants introduced entirely new racial casts to the American gene pool, and Hunter predicted that "racial modifications . . . are likely to result from the coming of these strange peoples from all parts of the world."[50] The connections, thus, were the alien, with the impoverished, with racial (genetic) decline.

When America embarked upon its "new frontier" and "new empire" in the Pacific during the late nineteenth century, during which America annexed and conquered the Philippines and Hawaii in 1898, and in 1899 it began its "Open Door" policy with China, when, in the words of Secretary of State John Hay, the nation's "Far West" became the "Far East," race, ethnic, gender, class, and ideological diversities had to be subsumed beneath the banner of empire. Imperialism bred conformity, not individualism. Hay conceived of America's imperial role in the Pacific as a trans-Atlantic alliance of the United States and Britain, as the bond of "the two Anglo-Saxon peoples" engaged in "the same sacred mission of liberty and progress."[51] Writing of this period and of America's pursuit of empire, historian Nell Irvin Painter noted "a vastly increased emphasis on race" that aligned white America with the European colonial powers set against African Americans and other peoples of color in the colonized world. Domestic divisions and expansion abroad, Painter observed, demanded "an identity as well as an identity of interest" that excluded America's racialized, gendered, and classed minorities and helped create transnational identities of white and non-white.[52] The Republic's diversity notwithstanding, the myths of homogeneity and a racialized order of "whiteness" contra "non-whiteness" at the end of the nineteenth century suited the allied purposes of domestic order and subjugation abroad.

That essentializing of whiteness, set against its nonwhite other, was imagined by British historian Charles H. Pearson in his tract, *National Life and Character*, published in 1893, the same year of Turner's frontier essay. Whites, he explained, had expanded to the farthest reaches of the temperate zones and, he noted, like Turner, there were no more frontiers left except in the thickly populated tropics, where black and yellow peoples lived and where diseases impeded white settlement. But whites, desirous of the products of the tropics, colonized those areas and introduced science and industry that not only enabled a more efficient production but also lengthened the life spans of nonwhites. The result, predicted Pearson, would be a huge population explosion among nonwhites accompanied by a rise in their power, and, led by Asians, the surging masses would challenge white overrule and spread into the temperate, white zones.[53] That empire that conveyed sugar and bananas to Europe and the United States also brought immigrants, prompting an anguished cry for simpler pasts, racial and cultural homogeneity, and higher fences to repel the immigrant tide at the end of both the nineteenth and twentieth centuries.[54]

Asian American history reveals a more inclusive and complex past than admitted by those nationalist, tribal, and introspective narratives. The familiar spatial dualisms of an agrarian set against a maritime tradition, the heartland as opposed to the coasts, and the Atlantic but not Pacific civilizations and their national, class, racial, and gender correlates and dualisms of American and European, citizen and alien, rich and poor, white and nonwhite, and manly Americans and feminine Asians, are false propositions and choices. Not either or, all of those spaces and social categories were formative and constitutive of the American character. America's very origins and its subsequent expansion, we come to see clearly through the lens of the Asian American subject, was the result of a transoceanic and transcontinental journey to India embarked upon by Europeans. Islanders washed by the Atlantic and the Pacific and touched by lands north and south, Americans were equally a continental and an oceanic peoples, both an Atlantic and a Pacific civilization. And the nation's borders, gates, and shores were more open and permeable than a moat and embankment would allow. Indeed, as Pearson recalled and foresaw, the European penetration and colonization of Asia motivated and conveyed Asian peoples to America's shores, and the influences they and other migrants brought to bear on the port cities and cultures of America's rim were as much a part of America's social fabric and formation as the imagined, less complicated frontier, where the environment was said to have shaped a singular "new man."

Geographies are neither predetermined nor fixed. The term the West, for instance, at different times and from various standpoints in U.S. history, might have designated the Americas, the lands beyond the Appalachian mountains, the Midwest, the Far West, North America, Europe and sometimes even Japan. We also realize that spaces, when marked by humans, carry socially assigned meanings. Thus, the West in American history was associated with vacancy, virginity, genesis, fertility, timelessness, fidelity, homogeneity, wellness, regeneration, agriculture, and plenty—in sum, an Americanism pure and undefiled. Like Dorothy's Kansas, the West is home. Spaces, thus, are freighted with significances that we ascribe to them. There could be multiple Wests, and multiple homes—West and East, the heartland and the coasts, rural and urban, field and factory, farmer and industrial worker. Must one or the other claim the solitary position of truth, authenticity, privilege? Could not both and all exemplify the "truly American"? Might not the contrasts be more imaginary than real, as in the land of Oz, or might there be commonalities in differences? And precisely where are the borders and barriers that distinguish and isolate farmer from industrialist, interior from coast, Kansas from Oz, America from Asia, West from East?

CHAPTER 2

White and Black

"Even with eyes protected by the green spectacles Dorothy and her friends were at first dazzled by the brilliancy of the wonderful City," wrote the author Frank Baum of the Emerald City of Oz. "The streets were lined with beautiful houses all built of green marble and studded everywhere with sparkling emeralds. They walked over a pavement of the same green marble, and where the blocks were joined together were rows of emeralds, set closely, and glittering in the brightness of the sun."[1]

The Emerald City, the radiant center of Oz, might have been Chicago for the book's author. Chicago, the hub of the Midwest and a sprawling metropolis, was an urban jungle to some wherein only the fittest survived, but it was also the site of Baum's home, his earliest writing successes, and his circle of friends and writers. And arising on the shores of Lake Michigan was a shining White City built for the 1893 Columbian Exposition, "the world's greatest achievement of the departing century," according to a Chicago writer and booster. The Court of Honor at the lakefront admitted the estimated 27 million visitors to the fair, and from that vantage the fairgoer could see a panorama of the grounds from the sculpture, water, and pennants and flags in the foreground to terraced lagoons and exhibition halls. Many people felt a surge of Americanism upon entering the Court of Honor, according to an account, from seeing architecture that evoked the simple classicism of Thomas Jefferson, to a sculpture that resembled the Statue of Liberty, to a dome that looked like the nation's Capitol. It was an American Forum to rival Rome's.[2]

More than a facade, White City was a utopian fantasy of sorts, sporting the latest in water, sewage, power plants, sanitation, and transportation. The streets of the city were clean and free of

Fig. 2. Court of Honor at the World's Columbian Exposition, 1893.
"I went to the fair at once, and before I had walked for two minutes, a bewilderment at the gloriousness of everything seized me . . . until my mind was dazzled to a standstill," wrote Owen Wister in his diary. "I studied nothing, looked at no detail, but merely got at the total consummate beauty and grandeur of the thing:—which is like a great White Spirit evoked by Chicago out of the blue water upon whose shore it reposes." Quotation from Alan Trachtenberg, *The Incorporation of America: Culture and Society in the Gilded Age* (New York: Hill and Wang, 1982), 218. Photograph by William Henry Jackson, courtesy of the Chicago Historical Society.

garbage and were patrolled by an efficient and courteous army of police. Drinking fountains were equipped with Pasteur filters, and a recycling system converted wastes into ashes used for road cover and fertilizer. The pavilions were a shopper's paradise, offering a vast array of the latest consumer goods, and along the broad, pedestrian-friendly avenues were coffee shops, teahouses, and restaurants. Circling the grounds was a raised train track on which ran America's first heavy, high-speed electric train. The first commercially successful incandescent lightbulb, patented by Thomas Edison in 1879, illuminated the fairgrounds and buildings. When the thousands of lightbulbs were turned on, according to a visitor, it was "like getting a sudden vision of Heaven."[3] Notably absent were the urban poor—the human refuse—and their associated filth, poverty, and crime. White City dazzled the Exposition's visitors, just as Oz's Emerald City had dazzled Dorothy, and it appeared to supply an antidote to the ills of modernity.

Although it celebrated the four hundredth anniversary of Columbus's "discovery" of America, the fair was more than a commemoration of national progress. As the Exposition's *Official Guide* noted, it was "a universal congress, which is no respecter of geographical boundary, race, color, party or sex. All the nations of Europe are bound to cosmopolitan America by invisible but indissoluble ties." European peoples, the *Guide*'s compiler declared, were bound together by blood and sentiment; other nations represented at the fair, such as Japan, India, Australia, Mexico, and several South American countries, were linked to the United States by parallel development and common destiny.[4] The exposition's cosmopolitanism, despite the fair's claim to universalism, however, extended only to European peoples and those who sought to emulate them. Though China refused to set up an official exhibit because of U.S. immigration laws that barred Chinese from immigrating to the United States, Japan was welcomed and given a choice location within the fairgrounds for its building because it had strived to show its desire to modernize its industries and prove itself worthy of admittance into the European family of nations.[5]

In truth, as if to confirm that limited view of civilization and of America's peoples, a section of the fair called the Midway Plaisance, devoted to Europeans, Africans, American Indians, Asians, Latinos, and Pacific Islanders, formed a connected but separate and discrepant attraction. The Midway Plaisance, the *Official Guide* explained, was not a part of the Columbian Exposition. Yet a path from the Woman's Building within the fair proper led hundreds of thousands of visitors from the exposition to the broad avenue of the Plaisance. It was at once close and distant. "The Midway Plaisance is a distinctive part of the Exposition," a souvenir book stated. "Although it is included within the jurisdiction of the Fair managers, it is very different in character to any other section. . . . The Plaisance is a side show pure and simple."[6]

Another fair guide offered a frank opinion of the distinction. "To pass out of the western portal of the Woman's Building, and to enter the broad, gravelled walkway which leads thence into Midway Plaisance, is the task of a moment; but in that time one is transported from the sights and sounds of modern civilization into a strange land, peopled with outlandish folk, echoing with barbaric noises, and given over to strange customs, costumes, tongues, diet, dwellings, and gods."[7] A history of the fair called the Plaisance a bewildering "paradise of Babel," and it declared that "there never has been seen such a mosaic, and there may never be again—not for many years, surely." The Plaisance's inhabitants, it continued, were a "fantastically picturesque mosaic of odd bits of tribes and nationalities from every quarter of the globe."[8]

Perhaps the Streets of Cairo, a popular feature of the Midway Plaisance, best represented the mile-long corridor that so fascinated and repulsed many fairgoers. "No feature of the Midway is talked of so much as the Streets of Cairo," a souvenir book claimed. "Grouped around the entrance are Orientals in turbans and fezzes and garbed in loose flowing draperies of gorgeous hues, that are sadly in need of soap and water. But the picturesque seems at all times in conflict with the cleanly, and soap is an unknown quantity in the Orient. Facing the smoking Orientals are two or three bright-eyed, half-clad, brown boys in dirty little robes and tattered sandals, busily munching slices of stale bread." Passing through the narrow, teeming streets, the visitor could but imagine the secrets hidden behind the doors and gates of the houses, and even familiar structures such as the Temple of Luxor, reproduced for the fair, were mysterious and concealed, recalling an Egypt "that lies buried in the dust of centuries."[9]

If the Streets of Cairo exhibit was exemplary of the spatial contrasts and distances between "modern civilization" and "strange lands," then the eroticism of Asian women's dances seemed to characterize the cultural gulf between the white fairgoers and the nonwhite denizens of the Plaisance. According to one account, the "loud rattle of the tambours and the shrill discordance of the Oriental lute" beckon the stream of curious patrons to a theater hung with Oriental rugs, tapestries, flags, and lamps, while musicians and dancers lounge about on sofas, and beating drums "stimulate" the dancers. The featured dancer, "a handsome Arab girl," steps onto the stage. "She is dressed in robes of red and gold, over which falls a shimmering white gauzy veil. . . . The girl has great black eyes and full red lips, and her small feet, clad in red leather slippers, are surmounted by graceful shapely ankles that peep out of her swishing draperies."

Besides the physicality of her eroticism, the "Arab girl" dances in a manner at odds with "normal" impulses. "The theme of the girl's dance is love," the anonymous author explains, "but it is the coarse animal passion of the East, not the chaste sentiment of Christian lands. Every motion of her body is in the illustration of her animalism, the languorous looks, the open lips, the waving hands, the swaying body, all are brutish; and as the shrill music passes into a noisy crescendo, the girl with undulating hips, protruding stomach, and wriggling frame, points towards the open mouthed Congo drummer, who shows his white teeth and red tongue and yells in chorus with the shrieking artists on the stage." The obscene dance reaches its climax. "Now the flushed face of the girl glows with passionate ardor, and she stamps her foot as she moves back and forth waving her beckoning hands. Then, in a perfect paroxysm of undulations, in which hips, stomach and torso are protruded and whirled, the girl rises on her toes and crouches in a series of wriggles towards the stage, like one in an epilepsy. Then the girl stops abruptly with a stamp of her foot, and the weird shrillness of the Arab musicians ceases." The dancer, in the words of another observer, trembled "with violent emotion," and her hips and waist appeared to "undulate and quiver in what might be called an ecstacy [sic] of delirious delight."[10]

Side by side, thus, at Chicago's 1893 Columbian Exposition, were two disparate yet connected worlds symbolized by White City and the Midway Plaisance. The former was a utopian vi-

Fig. 3. Asian Dancer.

"One more gorgeous Arab girl dances a measure, holding a sword in one hand, which she swings in threatening contiguity to the heads of her crouching, yelling admirers. The waving blades, the swishing robes and draperies, and the rattling brass ornaments make in the aggregate a picture full of color and novelty, and one that calls forth the applause of the audience of coolly curious Americans." Image and quotation from *The Columbian Gallery: A Portfolio of Photographs From the World's Fair* (Chicago: Werner Company, 1894), 4. Photograph courtesy of the New York Public Library.

sion, a model of modernity, a city of lights; the latter was ancient and dirty, a babel of decadence, an avenue of darkness. The contrasts were as clear as the choice made by some white women who, according to a souvenir book of the fair, would not enter the "Persian Palace" because their modesty "compels them to beat a hasty retreat."[11] And yet, White City and the Midway Plaisance were linked in ways that were more intimate than a connecting gravel walkway might imply. Their very differences were what defined them, what gave them their individuality; White City was what the Midway Plaisance was not. But just as important, they both embodied elements of attraction and repulsion. White City's sanitation system might have ensured clean streets, but it could just as easily have produced a stifling sterility devoid of passion or imagination. And the Midway Plaisance's sensuality might have indicated indolence and inertia, but it also exhibited intensity and a robust vivacity. Fairgoers, when moving from White City to the Midway Plaisance, experienced both fear and desire. As the souvenir book noted, even as some white women beat a hasty retreat from the Persian Palace of Eros, a "stream of men" moved upstairs to pay the admission fee and gape at the dancers. And yet another account observed that the dance "exercises a wonderful fascination over the spectators. They cannot explain exactly what it is that attracts them," the author reported, but all who had seen the dancers remarked that "to see them once is to long to see them again."[12]

Race constituted yet another salient bridge between White City and the Midway Plaisance. America's European inheritances and innovations were prominently exhibited in the structures and interiors of White City. African Americans were largely left out of those displays, and the Dahomeyan exhibit in the Midway Plaisance came to represent the deeds of black peoples generally. Noted civil rights leaders Frederick Douglass and Ida B. Wells published a pamphlet attacking the exposition as a "whited sepulcher," and they charged that African Americans were "studiously kept out of representation in any official capacity and given menial places." An African American fairgoer testified: "There is a lump which comes up in my throat as I pass around through all this . . . and see but little to represent us here."[13] In contrast to the displays of Western progress, the West African kingdom of Dahomey was depicted as a warrior society with gruesome and cruel ceremonies and even more hideous peoples. "The men are uglier than chimpanzees. . . . A more horrible-looking set of men and women it would be hard to find than these Dahomeyans," a history of the fair alleged.

As if to underscore the distance between European civilization and African savagery, Dahomey was represented as a deviant, unnatural society wherein gender and gender roles were reversed and women were manly and served as warriors. Dahomeyan women, the author contended, were "amazons" and "well-proportioned, clean-featured, muscular creatures, unusually intelligent for savages and possessed of phenomenal powers of endurance."[14]

Indeed, Dahomey was situated by fair organizers at the bottom of the rung, the primordial ooze from which humans emerged and marched from the depths of the Midway Plaisance to the heights of White City, from darkness to light. Frederic Ward Putnam, head of Harvard's Peabody Museum of American Archaeology and Ethnology, was hired to organize the exposition's anthropological exhibits, and the notion of racial evolution depicted at the fair thereby gained the imprimatur of science. The sheer scale of the fair's anthropological enterprise caused the curator of the Smithsonian Institution's Bureau of American Ethnology, Otis T. Mason, to declare that the exposition was "one vast anthropological revelation." The essence of that revelation, according to one of Putnam's aides, was "from the first to the last, the exhibits . . . will be arranged and grouped to teach a lesson; to show the advancement of evolution of man."[15] Like the exposition's celebration of the nation's four hundred years of progress since Columbus's "discovery," thus the "living exhibits" of peoples dressed in native garb, together with the material objects of everyday life that filled the exposition's streets and buildings, marked the races of humankind and commemorated their upward ascent. American Indians, accordingly, were exhibited as primitive peoples, but also as civilized through Indian schools managed by the Indian Bureau.[16] And progress was measured along the path that connected the Midway Plaisance with White City and by the distance between savagery and civilization, from nonwhite to white.

That studied design of racial types and racial evolution was not missed by fairgoers. A literary critic observed that the Midway Plaisance revealed a "sliding scale of humanity," from the

German and Irish villages at the end nearest to White City, to the center, where the Streets of Cairo exhibit and Asian peoples were represented, to "the savage races"—the Africans of Dahomey and North American Indians—at the far end of the Plaisance. "Undoubtedly," he proposed, "the best way of looking at these races is to behold them in the ascending scale, in the progressive movement; thus we can march forward with them starting with the lowest specimens of humanity, and reaching continually upward to the highest stage." The *Chicago Tribune* affirmed that observation in its description of the "living museum of humanity" along the Plaisance. "What an opportunity was here afforded to the scientific mind to descend the spiral of evolution," the newspaper exclaimed, "tracing humanity in its highest phases down almost to its animalistic origins." Those "animalistic origins" for most fairgoers clearly began with the Dahomeyans, who, in the words of a correspondent, were "blacker than buried midnight and as degraded as the animals which prowl the jungles of their dark land. . . . In these wild people we easily detect many characteristics of the American negro."[17]

Even as Africans were deemed to be the farthest from the European with few, if any, redeeming features, Asians were seen as intermediate, bearing resemblances to both the "savage" African and the "civilized" European. Asians were depicted favorably insofar as they approximated or were tutored by Europeans. The Japanese, called "the Yankee[s] of the East," were praised for their Yankee-like industry and desire to follow the European pattern of modernization. People from Java, or "the little people," were much beloved by fairgoers, according to a souvenir book, because of their "gentleness." Even their music was said to be soft and "always in the minor or sad key." Their Dutch colonial masters and the sponsors of the exhibit surely played a role in that representation of the Javanese as "a peaceful, agricultural people." "The women are pretty and at all times gentle and obliging," commented an author, and because the land is so productive the people "are naturally an easy-going, good-natured race, and inclined to a little indolence." But the people, under Dutch prodding, produced coffee and tea for the world market, and their participation in the fair was calculated by their masters to promote direct trade between that Dutch colony and the United States.[18] Like the Javanese, the savagery of the Samoans was held in check by the veneer of civilization brought to them by Europeans, according to a description of the fair's South Sea islanders. Thus, although their music was "rude and savage," its readers were told, Samoans were "a wonderfully good-natured people" and "simple, joyous children of nature."[19]

The ideas of race and human social evolution assuredly did not begin with the Columbian Exposition but had a long history in America. The disciplining of those popular notions, however, making them systematic, universal, and predictive—a science of race—was taking place at the 1893 fair and during this period of American history, the late nineteenth century. A parallel management at the fair, in concert with the naming and ordering of human types and cultures, was the control of space exhibited in the buildings and layout of White City. A model for the future, White City exemplified the melding of beauty and art with the latest in technological innovation all organized around a unifying authority. White City's (European) neoclassical buildings, declared the fair's planner, Daniel H. Burnham, were deliberately designed and grouped as high art to promote the notions of universalism, dignity and formality, permanence and monumentality. By contrast, Burnham noted, no distinct order was followed for the Midway Plaisance, "it being instead a most unusual collection of almost every type of architecture known to man—oriental villages, Chinese bazaars, tropical settlements, ice railways, the ponderous Ferris wheel, and reproductions of ancient cities. All these were combined to form the lighter and more fantastic side of the Fair."[20]

Like the science of race, thus, architecture and urban planning sought to establish within the senses of fairgoers the idea of a linear development and evolution from chaos to order, from simplicity to complexity, but also of a break and separation between the two supposed extremes of barbarism and civilization. Relatedness did not imply equivalence. White City might have evolved from the Midway Plaisance, but White City was not the same as the Midway Plaisance, or whites might have evolved from the lesser races, but whites were not the lesser races. Those were complex and difficult ideas, to believe simultaneously in continuity and rupture, sameness and inequality, because they seemed so obviously at odds with each other. Although science had provided a basis for a common humanity linked by the slender thread of physical evolution, it also posited cultural convolutions and paradoxes that apparently defied resolution.

That complexity was evidenced in the changing notions of race and race relations. The intention of Puritans to convert Indians to Christianity and civilization during the seventeenth century gave way to a hatred of Indians as agents of the devil when it became apparent that they resisted the appropriation of their lands and transformation of their ways of life.[21] And the eighteenth- and nineteenth-century romantic depictions of Indians as "noble savages" among intellectuals and writers in the Northeast was emphatically not the view of many whites along the expanding western frontier where they pursued the removal, if not extermination, of the indigenous peoples. George Washington likened Indians to "wild Beasts of ye forest" and to the wolf, "both being beasts of prey, tho' they differ in shape."[22] Even as nature's children and objects of admiration, American Indians were thought of as a simple race, arrested in development and forlorn in the face of industry, science, and modernity.

Segregation, like Indian removals, was a means by which some whites tried to distinguish civil from savage, white from nonwhite. During the 1840s and 1850s, there were various initiatives launched to keep the Midwest white. Indiana passed a law in 1851 prohibiting the entry of African Americans into the state, and Illinois similarly excluded African Americans two years later. Those already in the Midwest were encouraged to leave, and their colonization outside the United States was a popular proposal among certain whites. "Where Negroes reside in any great numbers among the whites," explained an Ohio newspaper editor during the late 1850s, ". . . both parties are the worse for it, and it is the interest of both that a separation should be made as soon as practicable." That desire to create racial homogeneity in the Midwest and install that region as a white preserve was widespread among many whites of the heartland, and fears of a black peril reached "panic proportions" after the Civil War with the prospect of emancipation and African American freedom. Whites imagined black hordes from the South streaming across the Ohio River and inundating the land.[23]

Like their fellow travelers in the Midwest, white nationalists in the North advocated the containment of blackness to the South and the division of the United States into a vast white region and a limited "African belt." As James Shepherd Pike, a correspondent for the New York *Tribune* put it, "Confine the negro to the smallest possible area. Hem him in. Coop him up. Slough him off. Preserve just so much of North America as is possible to the white man, and to free institutions."[24] More ardent white supremacists proposed the removal of all African Americans and peoples of color from the United States, thereby creating an all-white America. The 1857 antislavery book *The Impending Crisis*, written by a southerner, Hinton R. Helper, instigated a national debate, arguing that the color white was ordained by nature as "a thing of life, health, and beauty," while black was "a symbol of ugliness, disease, and death." Helper advocated the confinement of all African and Chinese Americans to reservations in Texas and Arizona, but he also was in favor of a providential design "to see the negroes, like the Indians and all other effete and dingy-hued races, gradually exterminated from the face of the whole earth."[25]

White disbelief in due process and equal protection for *all*, as promised by the Fourteenth Amendment, ratified in 1868, was in large part predicated upon that belief of white supremacy and black and nonwhite inferiority. That notion was given license by social Darwinism, which held that like the struggle in nature where only the fittest survived, in the competition between races, whites would predominate over nonwhites. The 1890 U.S. Census, the very same reckoning of America's peoples that had prompted Frederick Jackson Turner's ruminations over the end of the frontier, provided evidence to white supremacists of the veracity of their belief. Francis A. Walker, a northern economist and former superintendent of the U.S. Census, pointed out that the 1890 Census showed that blacks were increasing at lower rates than whites and that their geographic spread was limited to America's tropical, southern reaches. British author James Bryce exulted: "The census just taken relieves . . . a source of anxiety. It is now clear that the negro, regarded as a factor in the whole community, is becoming far weaker." And southern physician Eugene Rollin Corson, commenting on the 1890 Census, argued that the southward retreat of African Americans indicated their inability to compete with whites, and that the high mortality rate among blacks demonstrated their biological inferiority. African Americans, freed from the care and tutelage of whites, Corson maintained, reverted to savagery and were the hapless victims of "the struggle for existence against a superior race."[26] Some social Darwinists believed that, like the American Indians, African Americans were a vanishing race.

But the wish for the disappearance of nonwhites and white racial homogeneity was a fairy tale. It was as impractical as the colonizationists' schemes to remove African Americans to Africa or African and Chinese Americans to the U.S. Southwest, as childish as the monochrome greenness of Oz's Emerald City behind green shades. Excluding all Indians, blacks, and Asians was not an option. And America, in its rush across the land mass that was, it said, its manifest destiny, as ordained by God and history, conquered and absorbed Plains Indians, the Pueblos of the Southwest, Mexicans, Pacific Coast Indians, Spaniards, and Indians of the Pacific Northwest. The boundary between Canada and the United States was fixed at the 49th parallel in 1846, and the border with Mexico, in 1848, after a war and the Treaty of Guadalupe Hidalgo. Hawaiians were also numbered among America's newly acquired peoples and cultures. During the 1830s, Hawaiians constituted the majority of the crews of American fur-trading ships in the Pacific Northwest, and were widely employed at trading posts throughout Oregon country. They also worked as sailors and navigators along California's coast, and totaled nearly ten percent of San Francisco's population in 1847. Hawaiians worked on John Sutter's cattle ranch before gold was discovered on his property, and they married Indian women, established communities, and panned the rivers of California's gold country after the rush in 1849 alongside fortune seekers from the East Coast, but also from South America, Australia, China, Europe, and South Africa. A white man's country America never was and never would be.

And America, having reached the terminus of its continental limits and fired its furnaces of industrial production, launched upon an ambitious program of expansion and empire that snared an even greater diversity of peoples at the end of the nineteenth century. Underwriting that imperialist project were various interests, including desires for national greatness, for sources of labor, raw materials, and markets for American goods, for military and strategic advantage, and for new frontiers that would foster the American spirit of rugged individualism and free enterprise. The imperialists also drew from the well of contemporary scientific and cultural discourse, including social Darwinism and the social gospel. Perhaps the most prominent and influential spokesman for those allied doctrines was the Congregational minister Josiah Strong.

A midwesterner, Strong was pastor of a church in Topeka, Kansas. He exhibited the frontiersman's disdain for eastern capital and enthusiasm for westward expansion, and he merged the language of science with the everyday speech of small-town, rural America. His *Our Country: Its Possible Future and Its Present Crisis*, published in 1885, sold more than 175,000 copies in the United States and was distributed in Europe and Asia. Seizing upon the national anxieties over urbanization and industrialization, immigration and class conflict, Strong warned against the perils facing the nation and proposed a return to simple values and to the Christian reconquest of America. But he also found hope in America and its people, the Anglo-Saxons, who possessed the twin "great ideas" of civil liberty and "a pure *spiritual* Christianity." Mankind stood at a crossroads and in need of those virtues, Strong reasoned, and hence, "the Anglo-Saxon, as the great representative of these two ideas, the depository of these two greatest blessings, sustains peculiar relations to the world's future, is divinely commissioned to be, in a peculiar sense, his brother's keeper." The success of that mission, he assured, was mandated by science. Anglo-Saxons are a vigorous race, declared Strong, and they have created enormous wealth and exhibited a genius in the building of American civilization. "If I read not amiss," Strong prophesied, "this powerful race will move down upon Mexico, down upon Central and South America, out upon the islands of the sea, over upon Africa and beyond. And can any one doubt that the result of this competition of races will be the 'survival of the fittest'?"[27]

Strong's "Anglo-Saxon race," it should be noted, referred not to a "pure" Teutonic or Germanic strain, but to its American species, which was both a physical and mental adaptation and the result of mixtures of Europeans. White Americans, Strong observed, surpassed the physical stature and character of their European forebears, and "the marked superiority of this race is due, in large measure, to its highly mixed origin." Those origins included the English, but also the Welsh, Irish, French, Danes, and Germans, and citing Charles Darwin, Strong claimed that only the more energetic, restless, and courageous among them migrated to the United States. Hence, the remarkable culture of its white people was, like their genetic and bodily conformation, the result of natural selection.[28] Crucially, however, that category of whiteness, inclusive of several diverse European ethnicities, was not only the product of America's melting pot, heated by the miscegenetic frontier, but also the result of the repellent encounters between Europeans and peoples of color. Europeans became white Americans—Strong's Anglo-Saxon race and a chosen people—because they were not the uncivilized and heathen peoples of color.

That symbiotic relationship that created on the one hand a mythic white people and on the other an equally mythic non-white people was nurtured and redefined by successive migrations of European groups and their encounters with an increasingly differentiated racial other. Whiteness was not ordained by nature; it was created. And it was conceived in specific places and times, accounting for changes in those elastic categories,

white and nonwhite. Strong's Anglo-Saxon race of the late nineteenth century was not the Anglo-Saxon race of the English who
settled America in the seventeenth century. The first English
transplants conceived of Anglo-Saxons more narrowly, empha-
sizing their Germanic origins and their Protestantism. Superior
institutions, the love of freedom, and a pure Christianity were
the hallmarks of that mythical, Anglo-Saxon people.[29] Those
were the very white American virtues claimed by Strong over
two hundred years later, but they did not originally extend to
the non-English. Indeed, the Irish were, like blacks, bestial, simi-
anlike, savage, lazy, and sensual before the Civil War, and the
commonplace notion was that they were "niggers" inside out.[30]
The Irish became white Americans by eschewing "nigger work"
and Chinese "coolieism" and by embracing whiteness, and after
the Catholic church and Democratic party, both of which held
elements of proslavery and white supremacist views, extended
whiteness to them insofar as they belonged to the white American race that was, allegedly, a blend of the best of Europe.[31]

That more expansive whiteness resulted from Democratic poli-
ticking for the white vote in the antebellum North and in postbellum California, but it also emanated from a racist nationalism
that defined itself in opposition to nonwhiteness. Thus, it was
that in the 1850s Caleb Cushing could rise in the Massachusetts
legislature, in a state where a race riot in Boston had victimized
both blacks and Irish in 1829, to exclaim to wild applause, "It is
the Irish and Scotch and English and German blood of our fathers which constitutes our greatness, our power, and our liberty." That "excellent" whiteness, he declared, bestowed "intel-
lect in man and loveliness in woman" and the power and
privilege "to Christianize and to civilize, to command and to be
obeyed, to conquer and to reign. I admit to an equality with me,
sir, the white man—my blood and race, whether he be a Saxon
of England, or the Celtic of Ireland. But I do not admit as my
equals either the red man of America, or the yellow man of Asia,
or the black man of Africa."[32]

The Jeffersonian and expansionist Thomas Hart Benton offered a similar analysis of whiteness in 1846 when he included

the Irish in the "Celtic-Anglo-Saxon" branch of the white race. "I know of no human event, past or to come, which promises a greater, and more beneficent change upon earth than the arrival of the van of the Caucasian race (the Celtic-Anglo-Saxon division) upon the border of the sea which washes the shore of the eastern Asia," Benton declared. And he went on to delineate whiteness on the basis of its contrast with nonwhiteness. Asians, or the "Yellow" race, he argued, were once at the vanguard of civilization, but had become stationary for thousands of years. "It is a race far above the Ethiopian, or Black—above the Malay, or Brown (if we must admit five races)—and above the American Indian, or Red: it is a race far above all these, but still, far below the White; and, like all the rest, must receive an impression from the superior race whenever they come in contact."[33]

Europeans became whites not only because they, on the American rural and urban frontiers, adapted their "Europeanness" to their new environments, but also because they washed their ethnic colors in the bleach of nonwhiteness. And although the desire for an all-white republic was cooled by the attractions for nonwhite labor and empire, exclusion laws were instruments of population control, and segregation allowed for internal enclaves of white and nonwhite, of privilege and poverty, of two nations separate and unequal. While couched in the language of freedom and morality, the earliest federal exclusion laws failed to mask their underlying intention and application of racial exclusion and white supremacy.[34] The Page Law, for instance, passed by Congress in 1875, drew from the American well of free labor, but it forbade contract labor or work contracted for set wages and for specified periods of Chinese, Japanese, and "Mongolian" migrants. The law was directed at a classed, but also racialized, group of migrants. Further, the law restricted entry to women prostitutes and felons generally, but it was directed at Chinese women migrants and applied to them more for their race and gender than their alleged profession.[35] The 1882 Chinese Exclusion Act, similarly, was packaged as a law that excluded "servile labor" and thereby prevented the "debasement" of white labor, but unmistakable was the reality that with it, America, for the first time in its history, adopted an immigration policy that discriminated against a race, nationality, and class of people. In the words of California senator John F. Miller, a leading proponent of the legislation, the Chinese constituted a contrary race to white Americans. Chinese laborers, he argued, were "by long training and . . . heredity . . . automatic engines of flesh and blood; they are patient, stolid, unemotional, and persistent, with such a marvelous frame and digestive apparatus that they can dispense with the comforts of shelter and subsist on the refuse of other men, and grow fat on less than half the food necessary to sustain life in the Anglo-Saxon."[36]

Segregation enabled the simultaneous installation of white supremacy and nonwhite servitude.[37] Indeed, the segregation of African and Chinese Americans was coterminous and in several ways similar. One of the first attempts by California's legislature to exclude Chinese from the state was a companion bill to one barring entry to African Americans, and both were modeled on the black codes of midwestern states.[38] And when California's governor Henry Haight exulted over the Democrats' victory in his state in 1867, in the wake of the Civil War that had pitted whites against whites, and in the midst of southern Reconstruction, he urged the cause against nonwhites—Chinese and African Americans—as the vehicle to national unity. "I will simply say that in this result we protest . . . against populating this fair state with a race of Asiatics—against sharing with inferior races the Government of our country . . . and this protest of ours will be re-echoed in thunder tones by the great central states until the Southern States are emancipated from negro domination, and restored to their proper place as equals and sisters in the great Federal family."[39] During the 1890s, as if in fulfillment of Haight's exhortation for union under the banner of white supremacy, southern planters and industrialists united with workers as whites to dismantle African American gains during Reconstruction. White identity politics institutionalized segregation, including "legal disfranchisement, the passage of rigorous Jim Crow laws, new and more horrible forms of lynching, and a series of one-sided race riots which took a heavy toll of defenseless blacks," wrote historian George Fredrickson.[40]

Segregation instituted a rupture of the tenuous link of human evolution as presented at the 1893 Columbian Exposition, like the distinction made between White City and the Midway Plaisance. The border police patrolled the limits of whiteness and nonwhiteness. But like the two parts of the fair, whites and nonwhites not only lived side by side in each other's shadow, but were also related and intimately connected. Both the necessity for those patrols and the vigor of their enforcement assuredly testified to the presence and persistence of border crossers, those who defied the supposed natural order of things. The Irish lived and worked with African and Chinese Americans during the mid-nineteenth century, and they cohabited, intermarried, and produced biracial offspring who exemplified the fragility of racial fences and boundaries. In 1853, Irish and African American waiters in New York City formed a union and went on strike, and the 1860 U.S. Census showed that Moses Downey, an African American musician, rented space in his home to James and Mary Gallagher, an Irish printer and his wife. For nearly every example of conflict between Irish and African Americans, there were countervailing examples of cooperation, acculturation, and even intermarriage.[41] Chinese and Irish Americans likewise shared living and work spaces in New York City, and from the 1820s to the 1870s, twenty-five percent of Chinese men were married to Irish women, such as John and Margaret Huston, who, in 1855, had two daughters, Kate and Mary.[42] The Irish, both in their intimacies with African and Chinese Americans and their subsequent rise toward whiteness, clearly demonstrated the shifting tides and coastline of whiteness and nonwhiteness.

Because of its contingency, and because its meanings changed over time and space, whiteness (and its associated privileges) had to be constantly redefined and reasserted. As the African American writer James Baldwin noted, "No one was white before he/she came to America. It took generations, and vast amount of coercion, before this became a white country."[43] And

those processes of redefinition and reassertion pivoted, significantly not upon the alleged extremities of black and white, but
upon the equally invented polarities of white and nonwhite.
Black and white are, in truth, but two colors among many; nonwhite, in the end, is the negation of whiteness. That critical distinction was made over a hundred years ago by the chief justice
of California's supreme court in his 1854 verdict in the case of
The People v. George W. Hall. A white man convicted of murder,
in part on the testimony of Chinese witnesses, Hall appealed the
jury's decision on the basis that it violated the state's Criminal
Proceedings Act, which stated: "No black or mulatto person, or
Indian, shall be permitted to give evidence in favor of, or against,
any white person."

Among the several arguments he marshaled for his ruling,
Chief Justice Hugh C. Murray focused upon the "legal significa-
tions" of the words "black, mulatto, Indian, and white person."
The word "black," he conceded, was equivalent to "Negro," but
it also was inclusive of a larger group that was the opposite of
"white." The generic meaning of "white," Murray argued, excluded "black, yellow, and all other colors," and conversely,
"black ... must be taken as contradistinguised from white." As
nonwhites, he concluded, Chinese or Asians were among those
signified as black, mulatto, and Indian, and thus their testimony,
like that of other nonwhites, was inadmissible in a case involving
whites. Imagine, he mused, the "anomalous spectacle of a distinct people ... a race of people whom nature has marked as
inferior, and who are incapable of progress in intellectual development beyond a certain point ... differing in language, opinions, color, and physical conformation; between whom and ourselves nature has placed an impassable difference," deciding
upon the life of a (white) citizen and participating in the affairs
of "our" government.[44] The dividing line, Chief Justice Murray
affirmed, was what distinguished white from nonwhite.

Insofar as they occupied the critical borderlands between
white and nonwhite as plotted and defended by white supremacists and their allies, Asians comprised the crucial field of contes-
tation. Asians, it must be remembered, were situated at the cross-

roads between Europeans and Africans and American Indians according to the ethnography and architecture of the 1893 Columbian Exposition. Asians were near-Europeans in that they built, albeit in ancient times, civilizations, but they were also near-Africans and American Indians in that they were not endowed with, in Congregational minister Josiah Strong's terms, civil liberty and a pure spiritual Christianity. Because it conferred the rights and privileges of community membership, the acquisition of citizenship was the favored ground of struggle in the United States over whiteness and nonwhiteness. First specified in 1790, citizenship as achieved through naturalization was restricted to "free white persons," but the law was amended in 1870 to extend to and include naturalization to persons of African descent. Those limitations essentially held until 1952, when racial restrictions on naturalization ended. During that astonishing span of some one hundred and fifty years of the nation's history, most Asians were barred from earning citizenship through naturalization and therewith from the full enjoyment of life, liberty, and property.

Asians first tested America's racist definition of citizenship in a California federal court in 1878 in the case *In re Ah Yup*. One of three litigants, Ah Yup, was joined by Li Huang and Leong Lan in what Circuit Judge Lorenzo Sawyer called "the first application made by a native Chinaman for naturalization." In truth, though, several Chinese had applied for citizenship three years earlier in 1875, when Hong Chung, Chock Wong, and Chin Tin appeared before the California state senate to explain that they sought American citizenship because, in the words of Hong Chung, "American man make no good laws for Chinaman. We make good laws for Chinaman citizens." In the 1878 case, Ah Yup and his co-litigants claimed that Asians were included under the category "white," a strategy that was followed by all subsequent claims almost without exception, and Judge Sawyer, in ruling against Chinese naturalization, employed the argument that formed the crux of later decisions that the Chinese, by everyday speech and scientific evidence, were "nonwhite."[45]

Fig. 4. Race.
"It is a matter of no little difficulty at present to define exactly what constitutes an Asiatic type," confessed an account of the fair. "The various countries of Asia have been so over run by nomadic tribes and stragglers from every other country, who have become thoroughly intermingled with the natives, that there is hardly a definite trace of the originals remaining." Photograph (left) and quotation from *The Columbian Gallery: A Portfolio of Photographs From the World's Fair* (Chicago: Werner Company, 1894). Photograph (right) courtesy of the New York Public Library.

Between 1878 and 1909, American courts heard twelve naturalization cases that involved applicants from China, Japan, Burma, and Hawaii, along with two petitions from persons of mixed race, and one from a Mexican American. All claimed the cover of whiteness, and all were deemed to be nonwhite. Because of the Treaty of Guadalupe Hidalgo (1848), however, the "pureblooded Mexican" in Texas was allowed citizenship, despite the court's reasoning that science would define him as nonwhite. In contrast to the unanimity of the earlier period, the years 1909 to

1923 witnessed contradictory and confusing results. For the most part, in the twenty-five cases heard, courts continued to rule that Asians and mixed-race peoples were nonwhite. However, the distinction between white and nonwhite grew increasingly tenuous, especially in the light of disagreements over what constituted common speech, and its divergences from scientific opinions that themselves conflicted. Thus, Armenians were originally classed as Asians and hence nonwhite, but were rendered whites by a court decision in 1909; Syrians were considered whites in 1909, 1910, and 1915, but nonwhites in 1913 and 1914; and Asian Indians were whites in 1910, 1913, 1919, and 1920, but nonwhite after 1923.[46]

Armenians were rendered white by the court based upon scientific evidence, but Syrians and Asian Indians, despite scientific opinion that they were white, were classed as nonwhite because of common knowledge. The 1923 U.S. Supreme Court decision of the *United States v. Thind* codified that shift from both precedent and science in the matter of race. Bhagat Singh Thind was born in India, graduated from Punjab University, arrived in America in 1913, and served for six months in the U.S. Army. In 1920, Thind was granted naturalization by a district court based upon anthropologists' classification of Asian Indians as "Caucasians" and hence, in the court's opinion, "white." But upon appeal, that original ruling was overturned finally by the Supreme Court in a decision marked by a rejection of scientific evidence and an embrace of everyday speech. "It may be true that the blond Scandinavian and the brown Hindu have a common ancestor in the dim reaches of antiquity," wrote the Court in reference to scientific opinion, "but the average man knows perfectly well that there are unmistakable and profound differences between them today." The Court expanded upon its meaning: "What we now hold is that the words 'free white persons' are words of common speech, to be interpreted in accordance with the understanding of the common man, synonymous with the word 'Caucasian' only as that word is popularly understood."

Because of the *Thind* decision, between 1923 and 1927 at least sixty-five Asian Indians lost their American citizenships, which had been granted to them when they were classed as whites. One of those was Vaisho Das Bagai, who committed suicide over his denaturalization. In his final note, Bagai lamented, "But now they come to me and say, I am no longer an American citizen. . . . What have I made of myself and my children? We cannot exercise our rights, we cannot leave this country. Humility and insults, who are responsible for all of this?. . . Obstacles this way, blockades that way, and the bridges burnt behind."[47] And yet, despite the legal sanctions, racial classification sometimes hinged upon the capricious whim of county clerks who issued marriage certificates. Asian Indians were variously categorized as "brown," "black," or "white" by clerks who made those judgments based upon their perception of the applicant's skin color.[48]

Even as the category "white" was, in reality, fraught with ambiguity and contrasts, the class of "nonwhite" was similarly endowed. Persons were defined as "black," for instance, in Alabama, Arkansas, Tennessee, Texas, and Virginia if they had one drop of so-called "Negro blood," but Kentucky assigned that "race" to a person of one-sixteenth African descent; Florida, Indiana, Mississippi, Missouri, Nebraska, North Carolina, and North Dakota, to a person of one-eighth African descent; and Oregon, to a person of one-fourth African descent.[49] Individuals thus could be "black" in one state and "white" in another, or could change races by simply moving across state lines. The Treaty of Guadalupe Hidalgo that ended America's war with Mexico in 1848 guaranteed U.S. citizenship to Mexicans living in those lost territories. Mexicans were thus rendered white by an international agreement, but the Mexican American working class, especially throughout the nineteenth century, and Mexican Americans generally during the twentieth century, were deemed by social practice to be Indians and nonwhites.[50] Chinese Americans in Louisiana in 1860 were classified as whites; in 1870, they were enumerated as Chinese; in 1880, the children of Chinese men and non-Chinese women were classed as Chinese; but in 1890, those biracial children were reclassified as either blacks or whites, and only those born in China or with two Chinese parents were deemed to be Chinese.[51]

Besides those variations in the legal definitions of race, the racial binary of white and nonwhite induced divisions between and within both categories. The tactic deployed by Asians for the acquisition of citizenship, a quest for the mantle of whiteness instead of a claim to blackness, was understandable insofar as white supremacy ensured and limited rights and privileges to its members only, as was so poignantly revealed in Vaisho Das Bagai's suicide note. Nonwhiteness, Bagai knew, meant "obstacles this way, blockades that way, and the bridges burnt behind." But Asians, in their reach for whiteness, simultaneously sought distance from "the lowest specimens of humanity" that were, on the Midway Plaisance, West Africans and America's Indians. In protesting the 1854 *Hall* decision, a prominent Chinese American merchant, Lai Chun-chuen, wrote to California's governor John Bigler that "your honorable people have established a new practice. They have come to the conclusion that we Chinese are the same as Indians and Negroes, and your courts will not allow us to bear witness. And yet these Indians know nothing about the relations of society; they know no mutual respect; they wear neither clothes nor shoes; they live in wild places and in caves."[52] Although perhaps a reflection of his economic class, Lai's sentiment also appealed to alleged racial and cultural distinctions and hence privileges. The Chinese, Lai exclaimed somewhat incredulously, were not of the same order as American Indians.

Similarly, Bhagat Singh Thind's argument before the U.S. Supreme Court asserted that "people residing in many of the states of India, particularly in the north and northwest, including the Punjab, belong to the Aryan race. . . . The high-class Hindu regards the aboriginal Indian Mongoloid in the same manner as the American regards the negro, speaking from a matrimonial standpoint. The caste system prevails in India to a degree unsurpassed elsewhere." Thind's contention, accordingly, was that he was not only white but of the "Aryan race," that he was of "pure blood," that he was a member of a superior conquering group over primitive, indigenous peoples, and that he regarded the "aboriginal Indian Mongoloid" with the same disdain for inferiors that white Americans held toward African Americans.[53]

While some Asian Americans might have claimed whiteness on the basis of racial and cultural affinities, some African Americans sought distance from Asians on the basis of citizenship and history. "The Negro is an American citizen whose American residence and citizenry reach further back than the great majority of the white race," wrote Howard University professor Kelly Miller in 1924. "He has from the beginning contributed a full share of the glory and grandeur of America and his claims to patrimony are his just and rightful due. The Japanese, on the other hand, is the eleventh hour comer, and is claiming the privilege of those who have borne the heat and burden of the day." Unlike the alien Japanese, Miller argued, African Americans deserved America's promise of equality as citizens and as their "just and rightful due."[54]

Like whites, nonwhites were not all the same. The social determinations of race, culture, and citizenship ensured, if not encouraged, those distinctions, producing citizen races and cultures, such as African and Mexican Americans, and alien races and cultures, such as Asian Americans. At times, as in racial cuisines, race and culture were indistinguishable. In favoring Chinese exclusion, for example, a U.S. senator argued in 1879 that American manhood required beef, while Asiatic coolieism needed only rice. The former, thus, was expensive, while the latter, cheap.[55] Food ways or cultures were thereby racialized (and gendered and classed) as meat or white manhood against rice or Asian workers. They were also nationalized in that meat and white manhood were red-blooded American, but rice and Asian workers were alien and un-American. Racial (and gendered and classed) cuisines, in truth, are illogical. A dish or cuisine is not limited to a people or to a place. Asian workers can eat beef, and white men, rice. Race and culture are not the same.

At other times, all three social categories—race, culture, and citizenship—were collapsed as equivalents.[56] As claimed by a federal district court in the state of Washington in 1921, "The yellow or bronze racial color is the hallmark of Oriental despotisms. It was deemed that the subjects of these despotisms, with their fixed and ingrained pride in the type of their civilization, which works for its welfare by subordinating the individual to the personal authority of the sovereign, as the embodiment of the state, were not fitted and suited to make for the success of a republican form of Government. Hence," the court reasoned, "they were denied citizenship."[57] Because of their race and culture that rendered them forever alien, the court held, Asians were thereby unfit for U.S. citizenship.

And yet, from the Asian American racialized subject that is neither white nor black, we know that those categories of race, culture, and citizenship were ultimately invented and determined, as shown by their histories and legal genealogies, not by science but by the common speech of the "ordinary man." Race is not biology. Race is not nature. Race is not forever. Instead, "white" and "nonwhite" are what we, the people, believe them to be. And yet, although it is a conjuring, race acquires a searing reality through the weight of history, through the nation's laws and institutions, through popular culture and everyday practice. The entirety of those traditions has had coercive and liberating impacts upon our lives. But like the dualisms and contrasts of Oz and the 1893 Columbian Exposition, what appears real and solid might in fact be illusory and fluid, and the utopia of what lies just beyond, its light and beauty, its lushness and bounty, might already be within our grasp, within us. What is white in a place and time might be nonwhite in another place and time. There was a pathway, unbroken, that connected the Midway Plaisance to White City. And the dazzling greenness of the Emerald City of Oz and the whiteness of the fair's White City will appear monochrome, dull and gray, and like Dorothy we will come to see that there is indeed no place like home, our America inclusive of both White City and the Midway Plaisance, of all of its lands and peoples.

CHAPTER 3

Man and Woman

Situated on the borders of the 1893 Columbian Exposition's White City was the Woman's Building. Its location between White City, a shrine to the mind, and the Midway Plaisance, a phantasm of the body, was more than metaphor. It described precisely the place white women occupied in American society—in the spaces between white men and peoples of color. "That Midway is just a representation of matter, and this great White City is an emblem of mind," declares Miss Berry, a character in a contemporary novel about a visitor to the fair. "In the Midway it's some dirty and all barbaric. It deafens you with noise; the worst folks in there are avaricious and bad; and the best are just children in their ignorance." But stepping from that bewildering cacophony of sounds and alien sights and smells into the fair proper, "All of a sudden you are in a great, beautiful silence. The angels on the Woman's Buildin' smile down and bless you, and you know that in what seemed like one step, you've passed out o' darkness and into light."[1]

As if to underscore white women's borderline position between White City and the Midway Plaisance, among the displays and objects within the Woman's Building were not only the manufactures of whites but also of nonwhites, as a global collection of the deeds of women across races, classes, and cultures. According to the *Official Guide*, the Woman's Building was to be "a great museum or exhibition of everything that woman in the past had contributed, or is contributing toward the common stock of knowledge and material progress."[2] Thus, for example, the building itself was in the Italian Renaissance style, Queen Victoria of England exhibited six of her watercolors, and the sword and jewels of Queen Isabella of Spain occupied places of honor, but the office of Bertha H. Palmer, the president of the board of lady managers that ran the building, was decorated with the nets and baskets used by New Jersey's fisherwomen. Two Navajo women wove blankets in a living exhibit, and the needlework of Punjabi and Burmese women entranced the building's visitors.[3]

Despite their apparent commonality of gender, however, white women were not of the same class as women of color. Indeed, the fair organizers assured everyone, white women stood at the apex of women's evolutionary development, and the exhibits in the Woman's Building were presented to reveal just that. The Smithsonian's Otis T. Mason arranged an ethnological display of objects to reveal "a certain art" among "the three modern types of savagery, namely: the American, the Negroid and the Malayo-Polynesian."[4] He thereby hoped to show women's ascent from nonwhite savagery to white civilization. Likewise, murals by the well-known painters Mary Cassatt and Mary MacMonnies graced the building's interior court. On one end was Cassatt's mural titled *The Primitive Woman*, and on the other was MacMonnies's *The Modern Woman*. Cassatt's painting depicted women as oppressed, the servants to men's wants and whims. It showed a male hunter, just returned home from the kill, being cared for by a group of women and children, and centered in the mural were women—the burden-bearers—carrying babies and jars of water. In contrast, *The Modern Woman* stressed freedoms from the toils of labor and unrestrained opportunities. MacMonnies's painting showed a woman playing a musical instrument, another woman listening, and a third one dancing; women gathered apples in the central panel; and to the side, a group of girls followed by ducks pursued Fame, who was flying heavenward.[5] If the art was undistinguished, its messages rang loud and clear—modernity freed women from bondage, and white women were distanced from nonwhite women by the interior courtyard's span and opposition, from one end to another.

The Woman's Building and its contents, wrote a reporter, Marian Shaw, "signalizes the emancipation of woman, who from her ancient condition of disgraceful servitude, has risen to be the equal and co-laborer of her former master."[6] White women, nonetheless, despite MacMonnies's depiction and Shaw's hyperbole, still labored and chafed under patriarchy; and modernity, with its science and gadgetry, still bound women to the domestic sphere of home and family. In truth, most of the exhibits in the Woman's Building, of whites and nonwhites alike, emphasized women's roles as homemaker, nurturer, and educator. Colorado's entry featured a design by a woman for cooperative living. It envisioned multiple home units joined by a common kitchen and dining room, and was intended, according to the architect, to solve "the servant girl problem." Even the British queen's exhibit displayed the work of the Royal Red Cross and its nurses, whose instruments and bandages tended to the wounds of men, and in another section nurses with motherly affection ministered to dolls representing children in various stages of suffering.[7]

And yet, the intention of some of the women who had petitioned for and organized the Woman's Building was at apparent variance with those results. Because of an initial objection by women that their deeds should not be separated from those of men, women's works in art and industry were exhibited side by side with those of men in the main buildings of the exposition. But the Woman's Building was a special place that held meeting and reading rooms for women, and wherein everything was designed, built, or used by women. The hope, according to a historian, was to "clear away misconceptions as to the originality and inventiveness of women," and to demonstrate that women possessed talents and abilities "to surmount the barriers and limitations which have hemmed them in."[8] Women only won permission to actualize those plans for the Woman's Building, however, just before the opening of the fair, overturning the original intention for the building to be a mere annex to the exposition,[9] and the head of the board of lady managers, Bertha H. Palmer, prepared a stinging rebuke of patriarchy in her rousing address at the building's opening ceremonies.

Unlike the words in a poem by Flora Wilkinson that preceded the address, and that counterpositioned the deeds of Christopher Columbus and Queen Isabella—"He, sailing, and sailing . . .

[and] She, dreaming, and dreaming"—Palmer's words, as she rose to make her speech, declared that women too embarked upon uncharted waters and made discoveries equal to those of men. "We have traveled together a hitherto untrodden path," she noted of the board of lady manager's difficult efforts to secure the Woman's Building. "[We] have been subjected to tedious delays and overshadowed by dark clouds, which threaten disaster to our enterprise. We have been obliged to march with peace offerings in our hands lest hostile motives be ascribed to us. Our burdens have been greatly lightened, however," she acknowledged, to applause from her audience, "by the spontaneous sympathy and aid which have reached us from women in every part of the world, and which have proved an added incentive and inspiration."

Women's plight, Palmer emphatically declared beneath the paired murals by Cassatt and MacMonnies, belied the modernist claim that science had freed women from labor's bondage. The "few forward steps" taken during the nineteenth century through "the so-called aid of invention have not afforded the relief to the masses which was expected," she stated. Everywhere, she noted, competition was keen, urban and industrial centers were overcrowded, and the quality of life remained low. "The struggle for bread is as fierce as of old." She contended that women and children engaged in "the lowest and most degrading industrial occupations," and were not equally compensated for their labors to the great profit of the capitalists. Their struggles for survival and claims to justice were ignored as they had been for centuries. She observed that men theorized that women's place was within the home, ignoring the stern reality that women had been forced by economic necessity to earn for themselves their daily bread. "They must work," she said simply, "or they must starve."

Women, nonetheless, were not helpless. Indeed, the exhibits in the Woman's Building, Palmer noted, demonstrated "that ability is not a matter of sex." Woman "urged by necessity . . . has shown that her powers are the same as her brothers' and that like encouragement and fostering care may develop her to an equal point of usefulness." At the same time, Palmer cautioned, the planners avoided sentimentality by acknowledging that the "industries, arts and commerce of the world [had] been for centuries in the hands of men who [had] carefully trained themselves for the responsibilities devolving upon them," whereas there were but "a few gifted women" who had "rendered exceptional service to the cause of humanity." The head of the Woman's Building ended her speech, which was marked by spontaneous applause, with the hope that the exposition that had brought women together across national boundaries would contribute toward "a more lasting and permanent result through the interchange of thought and sympathy from influential and leading women of all countries, now, for the first time, working together with a common purpose and an established means of communication."[10] Palmer's internationalism that advocated a common sisterhood, however, contrasted with her deeds that included the appointment of a white woman to "represent the colored people" on the fair's board of lady managers.[11] Still, her trenchant critique of patriarchy—"even more important than the discovery of Columbus," she once declared, was the fact that the state had "just discovered woman"[12]—afforded a respite from the monotony of men's uncritical praise of civilization's progress and modernity's gifts to human labor.

In truth, White City was as much a paean to race as to gender; the grandeur that was White City was both its whiteness and its manliness. After all, it had been erected to exalt an aggressive capitalism, an age of steel and the robber baron, of cities and factories, of the Rockefellers, Carnegies, and Vanderbilts. Its architecture exhibited formality, strength, and size, and its massive halls featured powerful machines and engines, trains and warships, armaments and implements of war. The seven buildings—administrations, agriculture, art, electricity, machinery, manufactures, and mines—represented man's and civilization's highest achievements. Largely excluded from those displays, despite the best efforts of the board of lady managers, were the deeds of women. As observed by one of those lady managers, Rebecca Felton, "Everywhere the work has been credited to men. . . . The work of women in the farm exhibits is so intermingled and indissolubly joined to that of men, that we might as well seek to number and classify the pebbles on the shore."[13] And as if to confirm that distinction in the very architecture of the buildings devoted to the labors of men and women, the Woman's Building, designed by Sophia G. Hayden, was small, delicate, and plain. The *American Architect* journal patronizingly scored it as "neither worse nor better than might have been expected. It is just the sort of result that would have been achieved by either boy or girl who had had two or three years' training in an architectural school, and its thinness and poverty of constructive expression declares it to be the work of one who had never seen his or her 'picture' translated into substance."[14]

Infantilizing women's achievements emphasized their dependence, both real and imagined, upon men's works or the deeds of adults, and that contrast correlated with the distinction made by men between the provinces of the body and of the mind. Women and children, men commonly believed, were subject to the dictates and emotions of the body, while men developed and deployed their minds to control and exceed bodily limitations and passions. As was argued in 1873 by Edward H. Clarke, a Harvard psychologist, in his popular and influential book *Sex in Education*, men and women were endowed differently. He cited the example of a young woman who died a few years after having graduated from college at the head of her class. A postmortem revealed no disease in any part of her body, Clarke reported, "except in the brain, where the microscope revealed commencing degeneration." She died from "un-physiological work"; she used her mind, but failed to use her body. "She was unable to make a good brain that could stand the wear and tear of life, and a good reproductive system that should serve the race, at the same time that she was continuously spending her force in intellectual labor," wrote Clarke. "Believing that woman can do what man can, for she held that faith, she strove with noble but ignorant bravery to compass man's intellectual attainment in a man's way, and died in the effort." The education of women, Clarke argued, divested them of their "feminine attractions" and "feminine functions," producing a hermaphrodite in mind and inducing a "grave and even fatal disease of the brain and nervous system."[15]

The novelist Elizabeth Stuart Phelps, in a collection of essays assembled by the suffragist Julia Ward Howe to respond to Clarke's ideas, ridiculed the notion that women's bodies could not sustain intellectual activity. "Women sick because they study?" she asked of Clarke's contention that girls became sick or died after schooling. "Does it not look a little more as if women were sick because they *stopped* studying?" Instead, Phelps pointed out, a woman was made an invalid "by exchanging the wholesome pursuit of sufficient and worthy aims for the unrelieved routine of a dependent domestic life, from which all aim has departed"; she was made an invalid "by the prejudice that deprives her of the stimulus which every human being needs and finds in the pursuit of some one especial avocation, and confines that avocation for her to a marriage which she may never effect . . . by the change from doing something to doing nothing . . . by the difference between being happy and being miserable." Man, too, would be made an invalid, Phelps concluded, "if subjected to the woman's life when the woman's education is over."[16]

In truth, the contrary positions held by Edward H. Clarke and Elizabeth Stuart Phelps highlighted both the constructedness of gender and its contestations during the nineteenth century. Clarke's view—that gender, the ideas of manliness and womanliness, followed the dictates of nature or science—was countered by Phelp's rejoinder that gender was what humans made of it. The cultivation of the mind and women's advancement in education did not require a male body any more than it was a rebellion against nature, she argued. Rather, she contended, turning Clarke's argument against him, women's confining roles as assigned by men were what was contrary to nature. Bertha H. Palmer, head of the fair's Woman's Building, put it this way, to great applause: Women have "no desire to be helpless and dependent. Having the full use of their faculties they rejoice in exercising them. . . . Our highest aim now is to train each to find happiness in the full and healthy exercise of the gifts bestowed by a generous nature. Ignorance is too expensive and wasteful to be tolerated. We cannot afford to lose the reserve power of any individual."[17]

Palmer's feminism, nonetheless, was constrained by the impositions of gender's attributions. Thus, while arguing for greater freedoms for women, Palmer reduced the plight of women to her role as homemaker and life-giver—to "the struggle for bread." She declared that "ability is not a matter of sex," but she also advocated the education and training of women "for the factory and workshop, for the professions and arts, but, more important than all else, to prepare her for presiding over the home." The domestic sphere, Palmer stressed, was "the highest field of woman's effort."[18] Feminism during the nineteenth century could not, indeed chose not, to extricate itself from the separate spheres of men and women, the external and internal realms of responsibility and management. Still, as pointed out by historian Mary P. Ryan, from the sidelines women enlarged their sphere and created their own networks, organizations, and institutions that advanced their social and political causes without the interference of men. And white middle-class women astutely deployed their assigned status as mother and homemaker, and also as whites, to gain their rights as full-fledged citizens with the passage of the Nineteenth Amendment in 1920 and the vote.[19]

Despite the less than radical nature of the women's movement, many white men of the middle class believed their masculinity to be under assault from a variety of quarters during the nineteenth century. Historian Gail Bederman reviewed some of the causes for that disquiet. The economic depressions of the late nineteenth century led to bankruptcies and closures, and the traditional avenues for male status and power were disappearing. White women and immigrant men challenged and oftentimes beat middle-class white men in electoral politics, which formerly represented white middle-class rituals of masculinity, especially in urban centers of the East Coast. The middle-class white woman's movement for advancement in education, the professions, and political power threatened to erode the near-exclusive preserves of white middle-class manhood. "Between 1880 and 1910," Bederman summarized, "middle-class men were especially interested in manhood. Economic changes were undermining Victorian ideals of self-restrained manliness. Working class and immigrant men, as well as middle-class women, were challenging white middle-class men's beliefs that they were the ones who should control the nation's destiny. Medical authorities were warning of the fragility of men's bodies. . . . All this activity suggests that men were actively, even enthusiastically, engaging in the process of remaking manhood."[20]

Gender's constructedness was also revealed in the period's commonplace merging of race with gender and age, such that women, children, and nonwhites were dependents of white men and seemed to epitomize the frailties and whims of the body and not the discipline and logic of the mind. As was noted by the fictional Miss Berry, a character in the novel about the fair, the Midway was "dirty and all barbaric," and the best among them were "just children in their ignorance." Asians and Pacific Islanders embodied these convergences of race, gender, and age. The Javanese, reported a magazine, were cute, like children, and had bodily shapes that blurred the distinctions between men and women, and were, noted an observer, "small in stature, well-shaped, gracefully slender and erect in figure." Samoan men, according to an illustrated fair guide, possessed "a rather picayune style of manhood," and the women were "generally slight in figure, symmetrical, and easy and graceful in their movements." And although warlike and robust, Samoans seemed immature and addicted to drink, song, and dance that made them "as happy a crowd of South Sea Islanders as has ever existed."[21]

African Americans were similarly infantilized. Romantic racialism, as historian George Fredrickson calls it, praised African Americans during the mid-nineteenth century as distinctive from whites but with glorious gifts. Whites excelled in the arts and sciences or in "intellectual expansion," the romantic racialists held, but they lacked what blacks possessed—a "light-heartedness" and a "natural talent for music." Those milder, gentler virtues and childlike innocence rendered African Americans "harmless"; he "carries within him, much more than we, the germs of a meek, long-suffering, loving virtue," according to the writer William Ellery Channing. And as pointed out by Fredrickson, Harriet Beecher Stowe's wildly popular and influential antislavery tract *Uncle Tom's Cabin* embraced much of the rhetoric of the romantic racialists. Africans, wrote Stowe, were "so essentially unlike the hard and dominant Anglo-Saxon race," but showed "some of the latest and most magnificent revelations of human life . . . in their gentleness, their lowly docility of heart, their aptitude to repose on a superior mind and rest on a higher power, their childlike simplicity of affection, and facility of forgiveness."[22]

About the same time, expansionists who championed the cause of war with Mexico over its northern territories feminized its peoples whom they scorned as a "mestizo" or mixed race. Like the West's "virgin soil" that yielded to white men's implantations, a poem published in Boston in 1846 entitled "They Wait for Us," by an anonymous author, proclaimed the cause of America's manifest destiny in raced, gendered, and sexualized terms.

> The Spanish maid, with eye of fire,
> At balmy evening turns her lyre
> And, looking to the Eastern sky,
> Awaits our Yankee chivalry
> Whose purer blood and valiant arms,
> Are fit to clasp her budding charms.
>
> The *man*, her mate, is sunk in sloth—
> To love, his senseless heart is loth:
> The pipe and glass and tinkling lute,
> A sofa, and a dish of fruit;
> A nap, some dozen times by day;
> Sombre and sad, and never gay.[23]

Those complementary images of lazy, inept Mexican men and exotic, available Mexican women, along with the chivalrous and liberating white man, were habitual features of the American racialized and gendered landscape. The "Anglo-Saxon traveler" upon entering New Mexico, confided George Kendall, "feels not a little astonished at the Eve-like and scanty garments of the females he meets." Mexican women's bodies, he observed, exhibited "a roundness, a fulness, which the divinity of tight lacing never allows her votaries." Mexican men, by contrast, were unlike Mexican women, who were "joyous, sociable, kind-hearted creatures almost universally, liberal to a fault, easy and naturally graceful in their manners."[24]

Races were thereby gendered and sexualized. There were masculine races, within the American imaginary, and feminine races, and the men of the masculine races maintained sexual access to the women of the feminine races. The masculine races of both genders, the illusion ran, were manifestly destined by God and nature to master over and usurp the lands of the feminine races of both genders and to colonize them, to stir them from their slumber, for their animation and uplift. But those very notions of place and race and gender and sexuality, and their valuations that created hierarchies of superior and inferior, were invented and promulgated by the men of the self-defined masculine races and were not the mandates of either God or nature. And they sprang from the perceived needs of white middle-class men to redefine and reassert their manliness during an age when their assumed privileges and powers were being questioned and resisted. Imperialism and its raced, gendered, and sexualized missions, thus, were a means by which white middle-class men could recoup their social station.

Theodore Roosevelt, perhaps more than any other person of his age, came to typify those paired campaigns for expansion and remasculinization. Like the socially defined meanings of gender, Roosevelt's persona of manliness was carefully crafted and nurtured by him to advance his self-image and his masculine pursuit of power through a career in politics. A delicate, sickly boy, "Teedie," as he was called, appeared an unlikely candidate for the virile advocate of the "strenuous life" as a man. Indeed, the Roosevelt of the 1880s was lampooned by the press and his opponents as a "weakling," a "Jane-Dandy," a "Punkin-Lily," an effeminate novice in a man's world of rough-and-tumble politics. Newspapers ridiculed his high-pitched voice and tight pants, and some called him Oscar Wilde, the contemporary homosexual writer.

In 1884, Roosevelt moved to a cattle ranch he had bought the previous year in South Dakota, and there transformed himself into a masculine hunter and cowboy. "It would electrify some of my friends who have accused me of representing the kid-glove element in politics," he told the *New York Tribune*, "if they could see me gallop over the plains, day in and day out, clad in a buckskin shirt and leather chaparajos, with a big sombrero on my head. For good healthy exercise I would strongly recommend some of our gilded youth go West and try a short course of riding bucking ponies, and assist at the branding of a lot of Texas steers."[25] The "Cowboy of the Dakotas," as he called himself when he ran for mayor of New York City, solidified that image of manliness when in 1898 he served briefly as "Colonel Roosevelt," the much-publicized and fearless leader of the "Rough Riders" during the Spanish-American War.

Roosevelt was simply living out the imagery of the frontier, of the American West where white men—cowboys—exerted their powers over feminized Indians and the yielding, fertile soil through their hard and masculine bodies, but also over the products of their ingenuity—the gun and plough. Real Americans were thereby constituted on that proving ground of the West as men and as whites. Overseas expansion to other wests was an extension of domestic conquests. Western horsemen were long known as "Rough Riders" in popular adventure novels, and the connection between the Indian wars of the American West and the military campaigns in Cuba, Puerto Rico, and the Philippines could hardly have been missed by the public. Indeed, soldiers who had fought against the Sioux and chased and captured the Apache chief Geronimo marched against Filipinos beginning in 1898. And Major General Adna Romanza Chaffee, who in 1901 headed the American expeditionary forces in the Philippines, had spent decades fighting against the Kiowas, Comanches, Cheyennes, and Apaches, and it was said by his contemporaries that he "brought the Indian Wars with him to the Philippines

Fig. 5. Roosevelt and the Rough Riders.

"I had served three years as captain in the National Guard," recalled Roosevelt of his qualifications for military leadership. "I had been deputy sheriff in the cow country. . . . I was accustomed to big game hunting and to work on a cow ranch, so that I was thoroughly familiar with the use of both horse and rifle, and knew how to handle cowboys, hunters and miners. . . ." Quotation from Alexander Saxton, *The Rise and Fall of the White Republic: Class Politics and Mass Culture in Nineteenth-Century America* (London: Verso, 1990), 370–71. Photograph © Corbis.

and wanted to treat the recalcitrant Filipinos the way he had the Apaches in Arizona—by herding them onto reservations."[26]

Manliness was thus racialized by Roosevelt and his contemporaries in the conquest by white men of nonwhite peoples, both within and without the United States, and "westering" and imperialism or "the strenuous life" ensured the superiority of the white race but also shaped decadent, effeminate white men into paragons of virility and masculinity. Roosevelt's Rough Riders consisted of cowboys, cattlemen, ranchers, miners, blacksmiths, and railroad workers, but also choice athletes from Ivy League colleges. "They were a splendid set of men," Roosevelt claimed, "with . . . eyes that looked a man straight in the face without flinching. . . . In all the world there could be no better material for soldiers than that afforded by these grim hunters of the mountains, these wild rough riders of the plains." Although divided by class, those soldiers could unite as a race, as whites against nonwhite enemies, and as remasculinized men against feminized men along America's borders. And although American Indians and African Americans fought and died alongside his "splendid set of [white] men," Roosevelt questioned their manliness by noting that the Indians had been "civilized" by whites by attending "one of those admirable Indian schools" and that both Indians and blacks served under white officers, who held their nonwhite charges in check and ensured that they did not flinch under fire.[27]

Expansion and conquest, "the white man's burden" in the words of British author Rudyard Kipling, surely helped to reconstitute a robust white masculinity. As Kipling put it in his famous poem of that title, "The White Man's Burden," published in 1898 to prod the United States to take up the "burden" of empire in the Philippines:

> Take up the White Man's burden—
>   Have done with childish days—
> The lightly proffered laurel,
>   The easy, ungrudged praise.
> Come now, to search your manhood
>   Through all the thankless years,
> Cold, edged with dear-bought wisdom,
>   The judgment of your peers![28]

Imperialism, for Kipling, was both a matter of race and gender—the white man's burden. Expansion, nonetheless, was not simply an opportunity for some white men to search their manhood, it was also seized upon by some white women to construct and enhance their womanhood. As historian Peggy Pascoe has pointed out, Victorian women's status rested upon their moral authority, derived from their nurturing role within the family and within society. That role and hence authority, she reveals, were made prominent in the work of white missionary women, whose sexual "purity" contrasted with the "impurity" of Chinese women prostitutes whom they sought to "rescue." White women's colonizing project—the white woman's burden—assumed manliness in their "rescue" of "fallen" women and involved teaching Chinese women the virtues of Victorian female purity, Christian piety, and domesticity. Donaldina Cameron, the best known of those missionary women, was fond of saying that Chinese prostitutes were "the most helpless and oppressed group of women and children who live within the borders of these United States of America."[29] Certainly, Chinese prostitutes were oppressed, but the extremity of their condition and the social gospel embraced by the women intent on their rescue, also served to advance the moral authority and hence social standing of white women who labored in the mission fields of the American West and also overseas.

Nonwhites, indeed, simultaneously affirmed and denied white constructions of manliness and womanliness. By contrasts, feminized nonwhite men underscored the masculinity of white men, and barbaric nonwhite women conferred femininity upon white women. But the categories of "real men" and "true women" and their limits were thereby softened and rendered unstable. If men could be feminized and women masculinized, where was the distinction, believed to have been ordained by God and nature, between man and woman? If man was not woman, was not a feminized man an impossible contradiction? Race served to mediate that conundrum, to reinstall the gender fences, to explain how gender can form a straight line, but also be bent and made deviant. Race allows for normative and deformed genders, even as gender creates valuations of race such that masculine races were superior to feminine races. Indeed, as the presumed natural standard against which all else was measured, white men comprised the quintessence of race and gender, and nonwhites, as the negation of whiteness, constituted the de-

Fig. 6. Donaldina Cameron Cross-dressed as a Chinese Woman.

Head of the Presbyterian Mission Home for Chinese women in San Francisco from 1899 to 1939, Cameron, like a woman, delighted in being called "Lo Ma" or "mother" by the rescued Chinese women prostitutes, but like a man, she saved and held a patronizing attitude toward those fallen and helpless slaves and the Chinese as a race. Chinese women's prostitution, she wrote, "is born in their blood. . . ." Quotation from Laurene Wu McClain, "Donaldina Cameron: A Reappraisal," *Pacific Historian* 27 (Fall 1983): 30, 31. Photograph courtesy of the California Historical Society, Carol Green Wilson Collection, FN-24510.

facement of nature and those manufactured ideals. Thus, non-whites as races, and as men and women, were blemishes, stains, and deformities of nature. Raced and gendered, Asians embodied and exemplified those abstract concepts.

It is not surprising, accordingly, that some of the first Asians brought to America were exhibited as exotic specimens—aliens—for scrutiny by a curious and perhaps a trifle apprehensive public. Chang and Eng, the original "Siamese twins," were shown to eager audiences in America and Europe as oddities of nature. Born near Bangkok in 1811, the twins were joined at the waist by a cord that rendered them inseparable for their entire lives. Robert Hunter, a Scot and British trader, found the twins in Siam in 1824. When he first spotted them swimming in a river, Hunter described them as "a strange animal" with two heads, four arms, and four legs. He befriended them, gave them money, and visited their family for the purpose of exporting them to Britain and the United States to exhibit them. The king of Siam, too, had seen the benefit of using the twins as attractions when he included them among his diplomatic mission to neighboring Cochin China in 1827. Hunter took on Abel Coffin, an American trader, as a partner, and together they convinced Chang and Eng's reluctant mother to release her sons to them for two and a half years for $500, according to the twins.

In 1829, Coffin's ship left Bangkok, sailed into the Indian Ocean, rounded South Africa's Cape Town, and headed north to Boston. News of Coffin's passengers preceded the ship's arrival through the captain's letter to his wife. "Susan," he had written, "I have two Chinese Boys 17 years old grown together they enjoy extraordinary health I hope these will prove profitable as a curiousity." The day after the ship docked, Coffin allowed a writer from the *Boston Patriot* to see and report on the twins to generate publicity for his "show." "We have seen and examined this strange freak of nature," the reporter wrote. "It is one of the greatest living curiosities we ever saw. . . . They will probably be exhibited to the public when proper arrangements have been made." Indeed, the twins were shown to an eminent surgeon "to ascertain if there was any thing indecorous or fallacious in

Fig. 7. Chang and Eng With Their Families.

Katherine, Chang's daughter, wrote to her brother Decatur who was accompanying his father on a trip in 1867. "You said you was uneasy about home—there is no use for you to be so uneasy for Mama and myself will try and do the best we can & I think the children will do the same. . . . Tell Papa if he does not come home before the end of seven weeks that I do not think he will get many of the grapes to eat but I am going to save him some any how. I can put up a big bottle full in liquor & sugar." Quotation from Irving Wallace and Amy Wallace, *The Two: A Biography* (New York: Simon and Schuster, 1978), 255. Photograph © Corbis.

their appearance." Authenticated, the twins were subsequently viewed by thousands who paid fifty cents to see what the *Boston Daily Courier* called a "great natural curiosity."

Chang and Eng worked under Coffin for $10 per month and after two years, for $50 a month plus expenses, until they reached 21 years of age in 1832. They then insisted that they had fulfilled their original compact made in Bangkok and had become "their own men." By then, they had toured numerous cities in the United States and Britain, had made large sums of money for their "owners," and had "resented being in bondage, ordered about, controlled and driven by fellow humans," according to a biography. Recalling their period under Coffin, the twins wrote (they wrote in the first-person singular): "I am no longer a source of revenue to my 'owners' . . . altho' 'I have been bought' . . . yet 'I cannot be sold'; I have . . . to be thankful for continued good health & the prospect of still being able to do something for myself." After touring as "their own men," the twins settled in North Carolina in 1839, and proved their "manhood" by becoming landowners and slaveholders, marrying sisters, and having twenty-two children. As middle-aged men, the twins toured in shows organized by P. T. Barnum, who had begun his showman's career exhibiting an African American woman, Joice Heth, purported to be over one hundred years old and allegedly former nurse (she was a fraud) to George Washington.[30]

Barnum knew the public's fascination with "Oriental exoticism" when he founded his Chinese Museum in New York City, where, among other "curiosities," he exhibited in 1850 a "Chinese living family" that featured "Miss Pwan-Ye-Koo, aged 17 years. A young lady, with feet 2 1/2 inches long." She was, the April 21, 1850, issue of the *New York Times* reported, "a genuine Chinese lady . . . prepared to exhibit her charming self, her curious retinue, and her fairy feet . . . to an admiring and novelty-loving public." Sixteen years earlier, Afong Moy was perhaps the first Chinese woman in the United States, having been brought to America to be exhibited as "a Chinese lady in native costume," and, according to an advertisement, to show American women "how different ladies look in widely separated regions." Besides Chang and Eng and his "Chinese living family," Barnum also featured among the attractions of his American and Chinese Museums Chang-Yu Sing, billed as the "Eight Foot Giant," the "Man Monkey," and an albino family.[31]

Like the "living exhibits" along the 1893 fair's Midway Plaisance, nonwhite men and women were subjected to the gaze and inspection of white women and men. "Return as Freaks," read the *Chicago Tribune*'s headline over a story about a group of Potawatomi Indians whose ancestors had been expelled some sixty years earlier from Chicago, and who were members of the Midway's Indian exhibit.[32] Similarly, although they might have been men as property owners, Chang and Eng were less than men as Asians and as oddities of nature. When news of the twin's courtship of the daughters of Nancy and David Yates spread through Wilkes County, North Carolina, angry neighbors gathered at the Yates farm to protest the marriage of two white women to "freaks." They threw rocks at the Yates house and broke the front windows. Deviations from the norms of whiteness and American citizenship inspired a similar response. The Yates parents, reported a contemporary and friend of the twins, forbade their daughters to see Chang and Eng because of "an ineradicable prejudice against their race and nationality." According to a study, after the twins had married the sisters, Adelaide and Sallie, no one explained the unions as matters of love, but suggested that the white women were rebelling against parental authority, that they craved the attention derived from marrying a famous pair, that they sought the excitement of sexual perversion, and that they married for money.[33]

There were complications to this story of race and gender. Chang and Eng had, in truth, become two of the wealthiest men in the county significantly through the exhibition of their "unnatural" bodies. Their class status as landowners and slaveholders showed that unmitigated victims they were not. Chang and Eng actively participated in the enslavement of African Americans. Nonwhite solidarity was apparently not an issue with them. On the eve of the Civil War, Chang owned sixteen slaves, and Eng, twelve. Like members of their class, the twins reportedly whipped their human property, treated them with disdain, and disregarded their humanity.[34] But unlike members of their social class, Chang and Eng were, like their slaves, nonwhite. They were men because they were owners of property and had married and produced children, but they were incomplete or defective men because of their race and their freakish bodies. Adelaide and Sallie, too, were women, but they had been tainted by the stain of colored and "curious" men. Even their sexuality, although "natural" in that the couples were heterosexual, was deemed to have been perverted in many a discussion over how two men, enjoined at the waist by a cord that bound them together less than a foot apart, could manage sexual intercourse and maintain some degree of privacy. To neighbors and acquaintances, Chang and Eng introduced challenges and ambiguities into their imagined natural universes. They were free and propertied men, who were nonwhite; they embodied manliness as successful husbands and fathers, who were Asian; and, similarly, they were both successful heterosexuals, who were deviant.

Similarly, the "Chinese lady in native costume" and Barnum's "Chinese living family" raised questions. The spectators, white men and women, saw the Chinese as *not* white, while at the same time they created anxieties for them over their own images of womanhood and family and their naturalness. Were these Chinese not a woman and a family, and if so, could not woman and family be differently constituted? There were the familiar connections to whites—woman as object, woman as charmer, woman as costumed, woman as child. But there was also the unfamiliar—Chinese women with "fairy feet." Besides their infantilizing qualities, those feet held exotic promise to men. Not all women's bodies or their sexualities were the same. The custom of tiny feet had been created and shaped by Chinese men for their erotic pleasure. Foot binding, inasmuch as it was practiced among certain ethnic groups and social classes of Chinese from the twelfth to twentieth centuries, involved the breaking of girls' feet (along with their spirits) and the folding under of the toes to create the illusion of small, "fairy" feet. The process was slow and excruciatingly painful, and although adored by some men as beautiful, the bound feet crippled women, rendered them immobile, and made them dependent upon men as providers. Pwan-Ye-Koo's displayed feet two and a half inches long testified to men's powers over women in Asia, despite the men's diminished status as men in the United States. Asian men consorted with white men, as men and across racial lines, in women's subjugation under different forms of patriarchy.

And yet, Asian men, like the Samoans at the 1893 Chicago Exposition, belonged to a "picayune style of manhood." During the nineteenth century in California, Chinese men took up "women's work," because employment in many occupations deemed manly were closed to them. Thus, for example, although many Chinese men sought their fortunes in gold mining like other men during the gold rush, special taxes directed against them reduced their earnings, and white miners physically expelled them from certain mining districts. And because of white men's choices and the dearth of women, work such as cooking and cleaning and washing were open to Chinese men, who, according to a prevalent idea, were lesser men belonging to a feminized race. In 1850, the *Alta California* reported "much excitement" in San Francisco over the reduced cost of laundry from eight to five dollars for a dozen shirts, because Chinese men had joined American Indian women at Washerwomen's Lagoon. Twenty years later, most of the laundries in the city were operated by Chinese men, who also dominated domestic-service labor in the homes of the wealthier classes. "As a domestic helper the Chinese was an ideal servant and endeared himself to the members of the household he served," wrote Helen S. Gage in her memoir, "whether in a city, home, or on a ranch. He was completely devoted to the 'family,' as he called them. . . . Most of all, he loved the children. He was their adoring slave, devoted nurse, fun-loving playmate. . . . He hurried to their comfort if they cried. He would have defended them with his life."[35] Asian men's domestic labor, their "feminization," thereby helped to preserve and advance white manliness and womanliness, freeing white men from "womanly" tasks and allowing certain classes of white women to pursue opportunities outside the home, albeit a mere extension of their domesticity, and become what was called the "new woman" as complement to the remasculinized "new man."

Even Chinese men's appearance resembled that of women, according to some white men. In 1879, the writer Robert Louis Stevenson recorded his observations of America and its peoples. Among the immigrant "babel of bewildered men, women, and

Fig. 8. "Chinese Female Impersonator."

This man played the part of a woman in the "God of Heaven" performance at the Chinese temple on the Midway Plaisance at Chicago's 1893 fair. His dress and "shrill Chinese female voice," according to the photograph's caption, underscored the period's feminization of Chinese men. Photograph and quotation from, *The Dream City: A Portfolio of Photographic Views of the World's Columbian Exposition* (St Louis: N. D. Thompson, 1893). Photograph courtesy of the Marquand Library of Art and Archaeology, Princeton University Library.

children," he wrote, were the Chinese, whose appearance was repulsive to whites, causing "a kind of choking in the throat." They were of a different world, Stevenson commented. "They walk the earth with us, but it seems they must be of different clay." Those differences included a confusion of gender. "Now, as a matter of fact," allowed the observant Scotsman, "the young Chinese man is so like a large class of European women, that on raising my head and suddenly catching sight of one at a considerable distance, I have for an instant been deceived by the resemblance," although, he qualified, "I do not say it is the most attractive class of our women."[36] Perhaps Stevenson, like other white men, were disoriented by the Chinese men's loose flowing trousers, perhaps by their pigtails or queues worn as a symbol of loyalty to China's Manchu government. Those cultural markers, like Chinese women's bound feet, were certainly racialized by whites, but were also signifiers of gender. It is noteworthy that in 1873 a class of white men in San Francisco determined to punish Chinese men prisoners by cutting off their queues to an inch from the scalp. Although it was vetoed by the mayor, the queue ordinance was a symbolic castration of Chinese men, even as women's bound feet exemplified their subservience to men.[37] Chinese men's queues, however, were at once representatives of manliness (as phallus) and nationality, but also of femininity. Their forced removal, thus, might have signified both the cutting off of manhood and of citizenship to a foreign government and the defeminizing of Chinese men.

If Asian men's representations posed gender ambiguities, those of Asian women prompted similar anxieties. Not only was the labor of Japanese lower-middle-class women indistinguishable from Japanese men, reported the writer Pierre Loti in 1890, but Japanese men and women even looked alike. "The peasant woman, clad summer and winter in the same dress of blue cotton," he wrote, was "hardly distinguishable afar from her husband, who wears his hair in a knot like hers, and is clad in a robe of the same color." Indeed, Japanese women represented traditional Japan and the Japanese race for Loti, a race that with "ours" comprised "two poles of the human species." Japanese women, above all, exhibited the qualities of the people and their state in excess. They were, declared Loti, "small of body and mind, artificial . . . worn and aged in the soul. . . ." Japanese women were "very ugly," with "hardly any eyes at all, so little

Fig. 9. "The Pigtail Has Got to Go" (1898).

Civilization, depicted as a manly white woman, grasps and cuts the queue of
Chinese decadence and "worn-out traditions" with the shears of modernity and
progress. Perhaps the next steps in the makeover of the Chinese from barbarism
to civilization, from womanliness to manliness, might include a change of dress
and shoes, and the clipping of those long, sharp fingernails. Image courtesy of
the Firestone Library, Princeton University.

as to be almost nothing: two narrow slits, oblique and diverging," cheeks "swollen to roundness like a doll's," thick lips, and, among commoners, a flat and short nose. Aristocratic women, Loti distinguished, were bred "by fashioning extraordinary little artificial persons, with childish hands and busts, whose painted faces, whiter and pinker than a fresh bonbon, indicate no age; their smile is far away, like that of ancient idols; their updrawn eyes have an expression of both youth and death." Japanese women, summed up Loti, were childish, "very small creatures, living in the midst of trifles as artificial and light as themselves."[38]

Loti, nonetheless, was intrigued by Japan and spent much of his career translating its essence to an avid readership in Europe and the United States. Like woman, Japan to Loti was empty, invisible, mysterious, and hence intriguing, desirable, requiring explanation and possession. Japan's empress best embodied those qualities. "I admit that I plotted and intrigued to obtain my invitation from this almost invisible empress, whose very invisibility makes me dream of seeing her," wrote Loti of the empress's brief public appearance during the annual Chrysanthemum Festival. He described the moment when he caught sight of her under a parasol: "Her little painted face chilled and enchanted me. As she passes by, close enough to brush against me, across my chest falls her shadow, which I would have liked to keep as a rare treasure. I studied her carefully, and she is one of those few women who may be called, in the most refined sense of the word, exquisite. Exquisite and strange, with her air of a cold goddess looking deep within herself, or into the distance, or heaven knows where; exquisite, her eyes, almost closed, seeming in their length like two oblique black lines quite distant from those other two, more slender, lines of her eyebrows." Her ample garments, he continued, revealed nothing of her figure beneath, and when for an instant her eyes became "ironical, or hard, or cruel," they flashed "a cold flame. And she is more charming then, and more womanly."[39] The princess's manliness, her hardness and cruelty, according to Loti, made her "more womanly."

In 1871, American writer Ambrose Bierce published a short story, "The Haunted Valley," in the *Overland Monthly*. The story would reappear in 1893 in Bierce's second book of short stories, *Can Such Things Be?*, consisting of twenty-five tales revolving around the supernatural. The story's protagonist is "Jo. Dunfer," whose very name suggests gender ambiguity (even as Dunfer's house was called by the story's narrator a "hermaphrodite habitation, half residence and half groggery") and whose "most obvious characteristic was a deep-seated antipathy to the Chinese." Bierce made his reputation in San Francisco during the 1860s as a satirist and critic, particularly of hypocrisy and organized religion. "On last Sunday afternoon," wrote Bierce in his *San Francisco News Letter* column, "a Chinaman passing guilelessly along Dupont Street was assailed with a tempest of stones from the steps of the First Congregational Church. At the completion of this devotional exercise the Sunday-schoolers retired within the hallowed portals of the sanctuary, to hear about Christ Jesus, and Him crucified."[40]

In "The Haunted Valley," the narrator unravels the story of Dunfer, also called "Whisky Jo.," his (her) "pagan" cook of five years, Ah Wee, and a "queer little man" named Gopher.[41] Ah Wee's tombstone, engraved by Dunfer, presents the narrator with a clue and a mystery into the identities of Dunfer and his (her) cook. "Ah Wee—Chinaman," the stone read. "Age unknown. Worked last for Whiskey Jo. This monument is erected by the same to keep his memory green and likewise a warning to Celestials [Chinese] never [to] take on airs like Whites. Damn! She was a good egg." "It would be difficult to adequately convey my amazement at this astonishing epitaph," declared the story's narrator. "The meagre, but conscientious, description of the deceased, the insolent frankness of confession, the grotesque and ambiguous anathema, and last, but not least, the ludicrous transition of gender and sentiment, marked this as the production of one who must have been at least as much demented as bereaved."

Four years later, after the discovery of Ah Wee's puzzling epitaph, the narrator returned to the haunted valley, and there, next to Ah Wee's grave, was another, "a long and robust mound" that made the former "shrink from the comparison." The new tombstone bore the simple engraving: "Jo. Dunfer.—Done For!" The narrator's guide, the "queer little man" named Gopher, revealed how Dunfer had accidentally killed Ah Wee in a jealous rage over finding Gopher and the Chinese cook alone in a clearing one day. "Yes; Jo. thought dead loads o' that Chinaman. Nobody but me ever knowed how 'e doted onto 'im," declared Gopher. "Couldn't bear 'im out uv 'is sight—the derned fool!" Dunfer grabbed Gopher's axe and took a swing at him, but missed him, hitting instead Ah Wee "bad in the breast." Ah Wee gave "a little kick an' opened up 'is eyes—'e had eyes like mine—an' puttin' up 'is hands, drew W'isky's big head down, an' held it there w'ile 'e stayed—w'ich wusn't long, fur a tremblin' run all through 'im, an' 'e give a long moan an' went off."

By killing Ah Wee, sobbed Gopher, Dunfer, "that great broote killed the woman who loved *him* better than she did *me*!—me who had disguised myself an' follered 'er from 'Frisco, w'er' he won 'er from me at poker!—me who had watched over 'er fur years, w'en the scoundrel she b'longed to wus ashamed to acknowledge 'er an' treat 'er well!—me who, fur 'er sake, kep' 'is cussed secret fur five years, till it eat 'im up!—me who . . . fulfilled 'is only livin' request o' me, to lay 'im alongside uv 'er an' give 'im a stone to 'is head!—me who had never before seen 'er grave, 'cause I feared to meet 'im here, an' hev never since till this day, 'cause his carcass defiles it!" Ah Wee was a woman, who had lived publicly as a man, perhaps to escape the state's antimiscegenation statutes, perhaps to avoid society's racism. Positioned among two "lovers," the state, and desire (insofar as a slave's "choice" reflected desire), Ah Wee lived (and died) by cross-dressing, not in resistance to imposed categories of gender, but in resistance to imposed categories of race through a manipulation of gender's binary and a deployment of heterosexuality's privileging. Dunfer and Ah Wee, you see, could live together in the same household as men (or as women). But there might be another, perhaps more subversive reading of this text. "Jo." might have been a man or a woman. Dunfer and Ah Wee might have been lesbian lovers, both cross-dressing as men to manipulate and escape from the West's cult of masculinity. They were largely free from sexual harassment as men in a masculinist environment.

The very possibility of multiple readings of Bierce's fictional story of the supernatural arises from the reality that gender and race are constructions, performances, if you will. In that sense, "The Haunted Valley" is a very natural place where the mysteries are the creations of our own minds. Ah Wee dressed and performed as a man in the story, despite her biological sex as a woman. She was assumed by her contemporaries and her readers to have been a man, and was thereby treated as a man. At the same time, Ah Wee's performance was facilitated by the perceived gender ambiguities of her race. Asian men and women, according to some whites, bore physical and cultural resemblances. In their facial and bodily profiles and conformations, in their movements and gestures, in their dress and hairstyles, even in their music and arts, Asian men were feminized and collapsed with women, as a race. Ah Wee's gender trick, thus, was convincing only to those whose attributions of gender and race—Chinese men and women looked alike—were fixed and naturalized. Perhaps it is that recognition that is frightening in this tale of the supernatural, that the seemingly natural and stable categories of gender—of man and woman—are, upon closer scrutiny, really creations and performances, with faint and mobile borders that delineate them one from the other. Surfaces hide deeper truths, and those renderings, like the people who determine them, are situated in times and places and social formations.[42]

A common notion among European Americans during the seventeenth century, for example, was that women were sexually insatiable, easily given to temptations of the flesh, and thus suspect religiously. Men held contrary natures and controlled their sexuality, resisted evil, and thus were deeply religious. By the nineteenth century, however, white middle-class women were represented as sexually repressed and naturally spiritual, whereas men were said to have been ruled by passions and material, not spiritual, gain. Those reversals were dramatic and influenced by the shifting grounds of social relations that included the nation's impetus toward industrialization and modernity. The Asian American subject mediated some of those changes and showed how gender is racialized. White men's remasculinization during the late nineteenth century was achieved in large measure through the feminization of Asian (and nonwhite) men in the imperial project advanced by politicians like Teddy Roosevelt, and white manhood could be realized by expelling Asian workers, according to labor leaders like Samuel Gompers, president of the American Federation of Labor.[43] Analogously, white middle-class women were reborn and became new, modern women in the light of the Asian and nonwhite other, as illustrated by the MacMonnies and Cassatt paintings in the Woman's Building. Asian men domestics, cooks, and laundrymen, together with their subservient station, were the step stools that elevated white middle-class women; and white women's rescue of Asian prostitutes—a manly mission—enhanced their womanliness and virtue. The creations of the new (white) man and woman of the late nineteenth century, like the invention of whiteness in America, was achieved in part by the imaginings of difference across manufactured racial and gender divides.

Asians, too, constructed gender in the spaces of American cities and the countryside and in the contact of cultures. Chinese men generally avoided domestic tasks, and Chinese women chafed under the patriarchal lineage in China. Those roles and institutions were differently constituted in America. Economic and social necessity and opportunities helped shape responses that resulted in new gender formations and the meanings of man and woman to Chinese Americans. As noted by Lee Chew in 1903, "The Chinese laundryman does not learn his trade in China; there are no laundries in China. . . . All the Chinese laundrymen here were taught . . . by American women."[44] Conversely, in America, the patriarchal lineage was largely absent and was replaced by a network of fictive kin, such as associations based upon common surnames. (Having the same surname did not mean blood relationship.) There was, thus, greater stress placed upon the household and its lateral bargains forged between husband and wife instead of the vertical ancestral lineage resulting in a different kind of Asian patriarchy. And acculturation through missions, schools, laws, and social relations, and the more benign but pervasive cultural forms and practices of the dominant group, engaged and induced changes in the ideals and performances of Asian manliness and womanliness. Whether gradual or swift, gender classification was really a gendering for whites and nonwhites alike, a continual process of negotiation and re-creation.

But gendering was also and simultaneously a practice of racing. Their strands were braided, like a queue that marked gender, race, and nation all at once. If manliness was a quality of whiteness, then womanliness intimated nonwhiteness. Even white women, by virtue of their gender, were positioned at the racial borders, like the Woman's Building situated between White City and the Midway Plaisance. Still, whiteness conferred, indeed mandated, the distinctions of gender between man and woman as natural, as ordered, as certain. Nonwhiteness, contrarily, embodied gender confusions, of feminized men and masculinized women, of men and women indistinguishable and unnatural, disordered, uncertain. If Dahomeyan women were amazons, Dahomeyan men were of questionable design according to a *New York Times* account: "The Dahomey gentleman, (or perhaps it is a Dahomey lady, for the distinction is not obvious,) who may be seen at almost any hour . . . clad mainly in a brief grass skirt and capering nimbly to the lascivious pleasings of an unseen tom-tom pounded within. . . . There are several dozen of them of assorted sexes, as one gradually makes out."[45] Even the superfeminized empress of Pierre Loti's fantasy was "more womanly" because of her manliness, her hardness and cruelty.

And yet, the spectacles of P. T. Barnum's freak show and the erotic dance in the Persian Palace have powers of repulsion, but also of attraction. They can both affirm and deny. Like Loti's invisible woman, artificial and light, they demand capture, dissection, explanation—deeds of the mind and of man. The instructions for assembling man and woman are familiar and easy, like recipes we follow them, from cradle to grave. It is blue blankets for baby boys, pink for girls. But the gender ambiguities and alternatives posed by Asians and other nonwhites to the definitions of manliness and womanliness, like the instabilities they presented to space and race and the demarcations of West and East, white and black, reveal as flimsy falsehoods the presumed solidities of place, race, and gender, and lead us to the amazing discovery that beneath the hype of West and East, white and black, man and woman, there lies the reality that categories such as geographies, race, and gender are social inscriptions, contrivances, performances, patterns of speech, and what we, all of us, make of them.

CHAPTER 4

Heterosexual and Homosexual

"Down where the huge Ferris wheel blocks the way, there stands a building, square and ugly in its lines, surmounted by towers and cupolas, gay with gilt and crude blues," noted a remembrance of the 1893 Chicago Exposition. "Inside, the halls are adorned with rugs, carpets and tapestries, and sharp-faced Levantines and Orientals wrangle and bargain with the visitors over brazen chains and copper jewelry. . . . But follow the stream of men up the stairs, past the beady-eyed Armenian who holds out his thin brown hand for your money, and pass into the room reserved for the dances." In that "Persian Palace of Eros," the book's author revealed with feigned concern, "exhibitions of vulgarity" were performed by dancers with the sanction of both the U.S. government and fair managers.

Perhaps because of the "notorious" nature of the dance, the audience was composed entirely of men, "with a preponderance of college boys and prematurely gray men," who seemed eager to climb onto the stage with the women dancers, but were restrained by a stack of tables. In marked contrast to those sexually charged, if overwrought, white men was a jaded Asian man, a musician, for whom the whole affair was "banal" and "all the contortions of the girls have grown stale and unprofitable. . . ." Like the stereotypes of lazy Mexican men, available Mexican women, and energetic white men, that inert, asexual Asian man accompanied hypersexualized Asian women, who willingly displayed their bodies and performed for white men, who sat in chairs, smoking, laughing, and discussing "the dancing and dancers with startling frankness."

The Asian dancers were "very comely, but thick waisted and large footed after their kind, dancing with a grace that is heavy and languorous." The first dancer, the reporter observed, was "a handsome girl with a wealth of dark hair, on which is jauntily set a tiny silken cap" and who stepped forward to acknowledge her "vociferous admirers." The spectator's gaze was penetrating, as if seeing through her outer garments to ascertain her innermost emotions. "Over a blue silk bodice she wears a red silk jacket, and her loose red trousers are girdled at the waist by a gold and yellow sash," he noted. "Chains of brass coins hang from her girdle and heavy brass rings encircle the black hose at her ankles. Waving two scarlet handkerchiefs of silk, she moves slowly around, her white arms gleaming through her sleeves of gauze." Dancing, she seemed to induce sexual arousal and orgasm. "Now she revolves and turns, her face assuming a dreamy smile, her painted eyes half closed, her white teeth showing between lips made redder and fuller by art. Now she begins the contortions that mark all the Oriental dances; her movements are snake-like and vulgar, and she sinks lower and lower, wriggling, twisting, jerking."

After finishing, the dancer sits cross-legged on a sofa and smokes, as if performing a choreographed cliché. But there is more. The next dancer, also an audience favorite, is "not more than sixteen years old," yet sexually knowledgeable far beyond her tender years. Her dancing, the writer observed, had an unusual vivacity and was saturated with all the "vulgarity of all the lands throughout which she has passed on her pilgrimage from Persia to the Plaisance." After having experienced the first performance, the author sighed, one would have thought that all the possibilities had been exhausted. But this "lithe beauty with long, black, silky hair" exceeds all bounds of sexual ecstasy and excess. She "breaks into a whirling dance, and, gathering together the loose folding of her trousers, springs in the air and comes down on the stage in a shapeless tangle."

To an audience who had "cultivated an appetite for brazen indecorum" induced by these Asian women dancers, everything else along the Midway Plaisance seemed "staid and respectable," the author concluded, including the "frank nudity" of the Dahomeyans and Samoans, which by contrast appeared "refreshing and natural."[1] That vulgar sexuality embodied and exuded by Asian women had its attractions, but was at core repulsive and unnatural. Desire, the body, biology—correlates of women and nonwhiteness—had to be controlled, policed, circumscribed.

Indeed, as shown by those passages, space, race, gender, and sexuality were intimate and interwoven companions. The building and hall were saturated with Oriental opulence and intemperance; from its exterior towers and cupolas in gold and crude blues to its interiors of tapestries and carpets, the place was a shrine to indulgence. White men, presumably heterosexual, observed and so gained knowledge of Asian men and women and their sexualities. They dissected in their frank conversation the dancers and their performances and judged them with cheers and tossed cigarettes or quiet disappointment. Conversely, Asian women and men were on display as specimens; they performed, and in that exhibition of their raced bodies revealed their deviance as hypersexual women and asexual men. When measured against the norm—white men—Asian men and women exemplified curiosities and perversions of race, gender, and sexuality. As in a miscegenetic union between white men and nonwhite women, white women were absent from this narrative of eroticism for fear of contamination. White women's purity insisted upon their extrication from the pigsty of vulgarity. And yet, it is white men's privileges that are upheld in white women's absence, their possession over and access to white and nonwhite women alike.

White men's control over nonwhite women's bodies was perhaps most profound under slavery in the American South, where the lives of whites and blacks were closely intertwined. Southern white patriarchy mandated close supervision of white women's sexuality even as it promoted sexual license of white men with African American women. As Eliza Grayson testified, as a slave in Mississippi she had several children with men that she, as she put it, "have had to do" and as a result could not determine who their fathers were. Her euphemism suggests rape, which was common among white men of the planter class and their slave women. Such behavior was widely condoned by the shapers of southern society and was accepted as a way of life, although a few white planters complained bitterly about the lack of morals among men of their race and class. And a white woman expressed what was likely the general sentiment of her class when she warned against "the vile and bad habits of men."[2]

In truth, slavery and antislavery provoked images and arguments that influenced and justified behaviors between and among white men and women and African American women and men. White men's claim that black women were, like Asian women, sensual and hypersexual provided a rationale for their rape and sexual slavery. Samuel Cartwright, a Louisiana proslavery polemicist, depicted that Sable Venus when he spoke of "lewd and lascivious" African American women, who achieved "paroxysms of unconsciousness" and "vulgar hysterics" when dancing with men. Slaveowners' wives commonly held that black women were thusly predisposed, and displaced their anger over their husbands' sexual choices onto slave women. Some white women had the black women whipped, cut their hair to make them appear unattractive, or had them sold. Sometimes African American men also blamed African American women for their sexual bondage to white masters, and some African American women deployed their sexuality for their own advantage. When antislavery partisans decried slavery's immorality, proslavery men countered that the peculiar institution upheld white women and enabled her domesticity and softness, unlike the northern factory women. Simultaneously, slavery, its defenders held, uplifted black women from their moral depravity and taught them white virtues.[3] Mammy, that asexual domestic black woman, who, like Asian men, was a faithful family servant and nursemaid to white children, displaced Jezebel or the highly sexualized black woman in the pantheon of southern men's imagination, but was ultimately a creation and consequence of the system of slavery.

Property and its relations were surely the bases for white men's powers over white and nonwhite women. Ownership, whether as dependent child, wife, or slave, assumed those privileges of the master over his property. He could do with them what he desired. But those controls were mitigated to varying degrees such that white children and white women were afforded protections, both legal and social, that failed to extend to African American slaves and nonwhites generally. Those same principles were exercised in white expansion and conquest, wherein the conquered became the "property" of the conquerors insofar as they became subject to the new class of masters. And the white man's burden was not only a test of whiteness or of manhood, but it was also a display of white men's sexual conquest of and supremacy over their vanquished.

American Indian and Mexican women, as members of vanquished classes, were thus castigated during the nineteenth century as savage and promiscuous. "Cowboy lore in particular elaborated on the theme of the Indian whore, who 'lays on her back in a cowboy shack, and lets cowboys poke her in the crack,' " wrote historians John D'Emilio and Estelle B. Freedman. And white travelers, they reported, described Mexican women as morally debased and sexually depraved. At the same time, some white men claimed sexual privileges over nonwhite women as a right of conquest, such as the Spaniards who deployed rape as a means of subjugation. The practice prompted Pueblo Indians during the seventeenth century to petition the Spanish government for relief from soldiers who raped Indian women, and Indians complained of Catholic priests who raped their Indian servants. Likewise, American Lieutenant Colonel George Armstrong Custer, after winning a battle in 1869, allegedly offered a captured Indian woman to his officers for their sexual pleasure and selected for himself a Cheyenne woman named Monasetah. "In the predominantly [white] male mining areas of California, where local Indian tribes had been decimated by disease and impoverishment," according to D'Emilio and Freedman, "sexual contact between white men and Indian women usually took the form of rape, and sometimes paid prostitution." Besides conquest through rape, native peoples were also subjected to attempts to alter their sexual practices. Missionaries, for example, condemned premarital sex, "promiscuous" sex, and "deviant" sexual acts, insisting upon the "natural" or "missionary" position of man on top, woman on bottom, or active man, passive woman.[4] Besides curbing women's sexual assertiveness, the missionary position figured men's dominance over women.

Those sexual relations between white men and nonwhite women, nonetheless, did not comprise the entirety of the interaction. Some white men and nonwhite women chose to engage in sexual intercourse—fell in love, married, and raised families. Some nonwhite women engaged in relations with white men for gain. The relations of power of white over nonwhite, man over woman, were ambiguous and tenuous. And while some white men expressed apparent distaste for nonwhite women's bodies, others found them attractive. As a white settler confessed, the "Eve-like and scanty garments" of Indian women were a "little astonishing" and "really graceful, easy—ay, becoming." And although even less usual, white women married nonwhite men, such as Elaine Goodale, who married an Indian physician, Charles A. Eastman, and lived and worked on a Sioux reservation during the 1880s.[5] Those interracial sexual crossings, of course, held very different meanings and consequences for white men and women and for nonwhite women and men because of the different yet related hierarchies of race, gender, and class. White middle-class men, for instance, generally maintained greater freedoms than white working-class men or white women and nonwhite men and women of all classes.

White women's views of American Indians and Mexicans paralleled those of white men as whites over nonwhites, but they were also conditioned by their gender as women under men. White women were supposedly the moral guardians of the home and family, but they were also like American Indians insofar as they were both gendered as women and thereby classed as inferior, childlike, and dependent. Those white women who perceived that commonality with American Indians were more likely "to see native peoples in a more humane way than they had been initially capable of doing," according to historian Glenda Riley. At the same time, Riley cautioned, white women acted as whites, as a raced group, who claimed they were civilized and hence superior to the uncivilized and raced American Indian. "I long to be at my journey's end," wrote Sara Smith, a white minister's wife. "I long to be telling the dying heathen the story of the cross. O, how happy I shall be in my laboring for the good of those dear Indians. May God prepare me to do them good." Less tolerant was Sarah Herndon, who believed that American Indians were "the most wretched looking creatures" she had ever seen, "lazy, dirty, obnoxious-looking." Observed Riley of white women, "Their assumed superiority often encouraged women to emphasize, and indeed to even become obsessed with, the American Indian's supposed inferiority."[6]

The conversion of native peoples through the force of arms and the seduction of goods and social standing illustrated the constructedness of social categories and relations. Before European contact, several American Indian societies recognized elastic definitions of gender and sexuality and distinguished between them. Among some groups, women assumed men's roles, and in others, men assumed women's roles. "The Native American cross gender role confounded Western concepts of gender," explained anthropologist Evelyn Blackwood. "Cross-gender individuals typically acted, sat, dressed, talked like, and did the work of the other sex." These were not half-men and half-women as some European observers believed; nor were they effeminate men or masculine women. The cross-gendered woman was a man, who as a child played with boys, hunted, married a woman, and fulfilled male ritual obligations. Although gendered as a man, the woman was sexually rendered a homosexual, a lesbian, as opposed to one who was mimicking heterosexual behavior. But the cross-gendered woman's partner was always a woman in gender and sexuality and was not considered to be a lesbian or a homosexual. During the late nineteenth century, Blackwood reported, those mutable boundaries of gender and sexuality all but disappeared in the face of white insistence upon the distinctions between man and woman, heterosexual and homosexual. Thus it was that Sahaykwisa, the last cross-gender woman among the Mohave Indians, was ridiculed by Mohave men as sexually inadequate, and they teased her wife for wanting "a transvestite for your husband who has no penis and pokes you with the finger." In the end, a man whose wife had left him for Sahaykwisa raped her, and the people later killed her for being a witch, they said. "By accusing the cross-gender female of sexual inadequacy," concluded Blackwood, "men of the tribe claimed in effect that they had sole rights to women's sexuality, and that sexuality was appropriate only between men and women."[7]

Like those native peoples, whites delineated categories of race, gender, and sexuality that were contingent and socially determined. A history of sexuality reveals how categories of deviant and nondeviant behavior are created and change over time. The idea of the homosexual, as a social category, was only proposed in the United States and Europe during the late nineteenth century, most historians agree. Earlier, homosexuality was a sexual practice that anyone could engage in. There were no homosexuals. Everyone was vulnerable to the "sin" of homosexuality. But science, mainly medical science, sought to distinguish, classify, describe, and promote or remedy health and morbidity. That process paralleled other scientific projects at the time to name, order, and govern places, races, and genders at home and abroad. The disciplining of sexuality, like the science of race and gender, was conditioned by assumptions and values prevalent during the latter part of the nineteenth century. That was evident in the naming of homosexuality as "deviant" sexual behavior by medical scientists, who focused upon a range of deviant gender behavior called "sexual inversion" as early as 1870.

Sexual inversion included supposedly "passionless" women who assumed sexually aggressive roles. To scientists, that apparent reversal of women's gender and sexual character, as they defined it, appeared to be perverse and pathological. Victorian women, they believed, were as women and sexual subjects innocent, defenseless, gentle, and passive. Gender inversion thus accompanied sexual inversion and marked the lesbian who was rendered both manly and hypersexualized by late-nineteenth-century medicine, but it also identified a racial category, non-whites, whose women were described as like men and lascivious, even vulgar. As inversions, the lesbian and the nonwhite woman were gender and sexual deviants and hence in need of correction and cure. Men, conversely, who were classed as effeminate signified the homosexual man. When "the sex is perverted, they hate the opposite sex and love their own; men become women and women men, in their tastes, conduct, character, feelings and behavior," according to a study published in 1884.[8] And like the equivalence made between the lesbian and the nonwhite woman, the homosexual man finds correspondence with the nonwhite man, who is represented as gentle, passive, passionless, and asexual.

But those attributions of heterosexual and homosexual white men and women and sexualized nonwhite women and men were clearly situated in those particular cultures and times. We need only recall the cross-gendering among some American Indian societies of the nineteenth century or our contemporary images of men and women, straights and gays, nonwhite women and men, to recognize the historical specificity of race, gender, and sexuality. The concept of sexual inversion was peculiar to the late nineteenth century, wrote historian George Chauncey, because it was "a response to particular changes in and challenges to the Victorian sex/gender system such as the women's movement, the growing visibility of urban gay male subcultures, and the changing gender structure of the economy." To that list I would add the brew of anxieties over domestic ethnic diversity and overseas expansion. Medical theories simultaneously reflected and shaped those social situations and relations. "Indeed, the early biological explanations offered for sexual deviance were an integral part of that nineteenth-century scientific discourse which sought to validate the existing social order by asserting its biological inevitability," explained Chauncey. "Just as the contemporaneous theory of social Darwinism served to legitimate racism and colonialism by postulating a biologically-based racial hierarchy of social development, so the early sexology sought to justify the particular form of women's subordination to men during this period by asserting its biological determination."[9]

Even as race was linked to gender during the late nineteenth century, gender was connected with sexuality, and sexuality to race. There were masculine races and feminine races, and gender seemed inseparable from sexuality. "The genital and reproductive distinctions between biological men and biological women have been read not only as a necessary but also as a sufficient explanation for different sexual need and desires," observed social scientist Jeffrey Weeks. The selfsame biology that created the gender of man accordingly determined his sexual drives; likewise, women's bodies explained their sexual natures. Sexuality, he explained, was delineated by the assumed differences between men and women.[10] Further, as already noted, effeminate men and masculine women—gender inversions—signaled homosexuality, according to the medical and popular views of the late nineteenth century. And those discourses of science and common speech explained the popularity of black and white homosexual pairings as the substitution of race for gender. That is, although the couple was of the same gender, racial difference "normalized" the relationship in that the white man was masculine because of his whiteness and the black man was feminine because of his race. Likewise prison reformer Margaret Otis described the phenomenon of white women inmates who developed close, intimate ties with black women prisoners as "situational lesbianism" and the white women as "nigger lovers."[11] Racial difference thus substituted for and thereby "normalized" the absence of gender difference in sexual couplings, and gender inversions signified both homosexuality and nonwhiteness. In fact, miscegenation, a word derived from the mid-nineteenth century to designate race mixing, was applied during the late nineteenth century to both interracial and homosexual unions, thereby indicating deviance or acts against nature, racial and sexual.[12]

Long before whites fantasized over the hypersexuality of the Asian women dancers at the 1893 Columbian Exposition, the "oriental exotic, erotic" woman made her debut in the American imaginary. But perhaps the most immediate, most visible example of Asian women's bodies and white sexual fears and desires was the Chinese prostitute. Primarily a product of men's efforts, Chinese prostitutes were acquired in China and imported into America beginning in the mid-nineteenth century by Chinese men because the business was profitable. Those Chinese women were like the Filipino men who were impressed into sailing the Spanish galleons between Manila and Acapulco from 1565 to 1815, like the Asian Indian indentured man servants on board European and American ships that called at New England's ports during the eighteenth century, or like the Chinese and Asian Indian coolies, mainly men, who were brought to the Americas in a "new system of slavery" during the nineteenth century.[13] Procurers bought, kidnapped, tricked, and coerced Chinese women and girls in their teens into sex work in California and the American West as early as 1849. The women's stories reveal some of the aspects of that traffic.

"I was brought here eighteen months ago," began a woman in an article published in February 1892, "and am twenty years old. I was kidnapped in China and brought over here. The man who kidnapped me sold me for four hundred dollars to a San Francisco slave-dealer; and he sold me here for seventeen hundred dollars. I have been a brothel slave ever since." Another recalled how she had been deceived by a promise of marriage. "I am sixteen years old; was born in Canton," she began. "My father died when I was two years old, and left my mother and me and a little brother with no one to support us. My mother worked hard as a seamstress, and I helped her when I got older. When I was fifteen years of age arrangements were made for my marriage, and I was betrothed to a man in Hong Kong." One day, a woman emissary from her fiancé arrived at her home and took her to a ship that, she assured her, would take her to her future husband. "There was a man on board who all the time was teaching me what to say. He coaxed me to be quiet, and told me I would have a rich husband and a fine time in California." The man threatened the teenager with imprisonment if she failed to cooperate, and after clearing immigration, she was sold for $1530 and forced to work as a prostitute. "They forced me to do their bidding, but I cried and resisted. I did not want to lead this life.

They starved me for days, tying me where food was almost in reach of me. . . . Then they beat me time after time, and threatened to kill me if I did not behave right."[14]

Like the Asian men indentures of this period, Chinese women prostitutes, usually under duress, "signed" contracts that outlined the terms of their bondage. Protestant missionary Otis Gibson obtained and translated a contract dated October 1873.

> AN AGREEMENT to assist the woman Ah Ho, because coming from   China to San Francisco she became indebted to her mistress for passage. Ah Ho herself asks Mr. Yee Kwan to advance for her six hundred and thirty dollars, for which Ah Ho distinctly agrees to give her body to Mr. Yee for service as a prostitute for a term of four years. There shall be no interest on the money. Ah Ho shall receive no wages. At the expiration of four years Ah Ho shall be her own master. Mr. Yee Kwan shall not hinder nor trouble her. If Ah Ho runs away before her time is out, her mistress shall find her and return her, and whatever expense is incurred in finding and returning her, Ah Ho shall pay. On this day of agreement Ah Ho with her own hands has received from Mr. Yee Kwan six hundred and thirty dollars. If Ah Ho shall be sick at any time for more than ten days, she shall make up by an extra month of service for every ten days of sickness. Now this agreement has proof—this paper received by Ah Ho is witness.[15]

The contract reveals as much as it hides. The provision, for example, covering the costs of Ah Ho's possible escape was included in the document because Chinese women commonly tried to flee from prostitution. And the requirement to provide a month of additional service for every ten days of sickness amounted to a lifetime of servitude instead of the four-year term specified in the contract, because anything that prevented sexual labor, such as menses, pregnancies, or illnesses, counted as sick days. At this prostitution's peak between 1852 and 1873, according to an estimate, the major conveyer of Chinese prostitutes made $200,000 by importing about 6,000 women or 87 percent of all Chinese women migrants to America. Also receiving profits from the trade were procurers and the American consulate in China, shippers, immigration officials in the United States, police officers, and landlords—nearly all men and including both Chinese and white.[16]

Chinese women sex workers, unlike most of their white counterparts, were rarely free to pursue their profession as individuals. Exceptional, thus, was Ah Toy, a prostitute who was probably the best known Chinese woman of her time in the American West. Ah Toy arrived in California from Hong Kong in 1849 as a twenty-year-old to "better her condition," according to an account of her testimony in court. She was hugely successful, in part because of her physical appearance, but also because she astutely played upon a myth of Asian women's sexuality. White men described her as tall and with bound feet, and one wrote of her in 1851 as "the strangely alluring Achoy, with her slender body and laughing eyes." The line of men outside her place of business, it was said, sometimes extended a block long, and "whenever a boat from Sacramento docked, the miners would break into a run for Ah Toy's."[17] The "strangely alluring" Ah Toy created a special market for herself and for the prostitutes she imported as a madam by promising white men that Asian women's vaginas differed from those of white women. As one of Ah Toy's former prostitutes put it, "You hear hey, all Chinese girls they have cunt go east-west, not north-south like white girls hey, you hear?" Pandering to white men's racial and sexual fantasy, Ah Toy charged them for looking at her body and charged them even more for having sex with a Chinese woman or a racialized woman with allegedly different sex parts and hence talents. A white former prostitute and madam, Nell Kimball, admiringly described Ah Toy's gambit and the selling of racialized sex as using "her head as well as what she sat on." Ah Toy and the Chinese prostitutes who followed her, she explained, created and offered an illusion, "a white man's idea of China, all in musk, sandlewood [sic], teak, silk hangings, gods, scrolls and wall paintings. A parlor house had from six to twenty-four girls in Oriental costume, hair piled up and shiny, ready to be treated as a slave or toy."[18]

Chinese men visited Chinese prostitutes for companionship and sex. Ah Quin, for instance, wrote in his diary that he patronized brothels to "rest," although he was clearly angry when he wrote on January 25, 1880, after having visited a brothel: "A bad Chinese woman [in the] room, only fuck once. So mad [at] her."[19] White men sought out Chinese prostitutes for sex but also for their race. And those renderings of both sex and race—racialized sex—by white men and Chinese women, were as much in the head as in the sex organs. "It's amazing the idea you can sell a man about fornication—he'll pay and even if fooled, feel at least he's gotten some knowledge or experience," declared Kimball, the white ex-madam. Chinese men, like white men, were drawn across the imagined racial divide because of sexual fantasy, but also, unlike white men, because of an accompanying rise in social status. "Rich Chinamen liked to cross the color line," recalled Kimball. "John Chinaman has a yen for having ten or twelve women at hand if he can afford it. One or two white ones give him a feeling he's done well." Kimball's racism notwithstanding, racialized sex held different meanings and consequences for white and Chinese men and women. Moreover, racialized sex conjured up stereotypes of gender and gender relations. "Chinamen like a girl who is placid," Kimball asserted, "as if in a pantomime, she doesn't hardly look up at his face, and doesn't mind being given a knock, a cuff . . . a Chinese girl respects a man for being a superior being and a master."[20] Race, gender, and sexuality form a single cluster of discrete, yet overlapping categories when we think about an Asian woman's sexuality or a white man's sexual fascination for an Asian woman's body or an Asian man's sexual desire for a white woman.

Even as Chinese women were hypersexualized by whites, usually men, Chinese men were rendered asexual. Within the white imaginary, short, diminutive, childlike men represented small, stunted, immature sexualities. These men preyed on children because they lacked the manliness to woo and win grown women. "The worst bastards with women, girl-children" wrote Nell Kimball, "were the Chinese [men]. They brought young girls over like chickens in cages. . . . One load had 44 girls from eight to

Fig. 10. Scenes of Sexual Anxiety (1868, 1883).

A Chinese man lures white children with his candy, and a Chinese man serves up opium to white women. Presumed predators of children and women, lesser Asian men used sweets and dope to compensate for their inadequacies to seduce their victims. "Chinese Candy Seller," *Harper's Weekly*, September 19, 1868, courtesy HarpWeek LLD. "Opium Smokers," *Frank Leslie's Illustrated*, May 12, 1883, courtesy of the Wong Ching Foo Collection.

thirteen years of age." Chinese men found white women uncontrollable, Kimball continued, because white women were naturally feisty and independent-minded. To make them manageable, she alleged, Chinese men plied white women with drugs. "The truth was they [Chinese men] always tried to get the white kid tied on the smoke, opium," declared Kimball. "Then they'd take her away and set her up as a concubine in some cellar dive. . . . The women all had small rooms with bars on the windows."[21] Deficient with and not man enough for white women, implied Kimball, Chinese men had to compensate by resorting to dope.

Even the champions of the Chinese, perhaps in response to the charge that sexual deviance was endemic to the race, depicted Chinese men as docile, feminine, and asexual. Mary Roberts Coolidge, a sociologist whose 1909 book *Chinese Immigration* was written to argue against Chinese exclusion, described Chinese men as being of an alien race and an indeterminate gender. "With physical and social characteristics so different from the rest of the population it was, perhaps, inevitable that the Chinaman with his flowing trousers and queue should be a conspicuous mark for race persecution in California at a time when the feeling against all foreigners was very strong," she wrote. But Chinese men's gender ambiguity with their "flowing trousers" and queues, argued Coolidge, indeed their feminization, made them welcome additions to the state's labor force. "The cleanliness, unobtrusiveness and industry of the Chinese was often commented upon," she noted. "As cooks and laundrymen they supplied the places of women domestics." Even in mining, requiring rough masculine labor, Chinese men were unaggressive as competitors or in staking claims, and "they were said to handle tools like women and to expend a vast deal of labor in their method of working." Words like systematic, steady, timid, quiet, and inoffensive were used to describe those Chinese miners. A correlate of Chinese men's feminization was their alleged asexuality, described suggestively by Coolidge: "There are hundreds of [white] women on lonely ranches who have been indebted to Chinamen for their safety, their comfort, even for nursing of themselves and children when no other help was to be had; for in the country districts, the only common man with whom as a class, a [white] woman is perfectly safe is the Chinaman."[22]

Coolidge's portrayal of Chinese men at the turn of the century is drawn from the same trove of romantic racialism that moved antislavery writers during the mid-nineteenth century. African Americans, unlike the hard and masculine "Anglo-Saxon race," those polemicists declared, were mild and gentle and childlike. They were harmless and lowly, long-suffering and docile. They were, as a race, feminine; and as women, of diminished sexual longings and aggressions. Coolidge's Chinese men were of like constitution, and Chinese women, too, moved from the ranks of the lewd and lascivious to the victimized and helpless. In truth, much of the campaign against Chinese women's prostitution was shaped by the rhetoric of the abolitionist movement. Chinese prostitutes were referred to as slaves, in narratives such as

Mary Grace Edholm's broadside against Chinese prostitution, and the traffic was declared to be a new form of slavery, "slavery so vile and debasing that all the horrors of negro American slavery do not begin to compare with it," in her hyperbolic words. Chinese prostitution was "child slavery," the practice was immoral, and its victims cried out to white reformers for help. "One such Chinese woman, with her little girl of six years of age," wrote Edholm, "with a frightened, hunted look, begged the protection of the 'Jesus women,' as they called the Methodist Mission." As if to underscore the feminine position of Chinese prostitutes and the masculine role of their white mission women defenders, Edholm described the "motherly rescuers" as "most manly." "These girls revolt at their horrible lives," Edholm concluded. "But what choice have slaves? Let America blot out yellow slavery. Let the Chinese woman as well as the African man point to the stars and stripes and say, No man dares do me injustice under this flag."[23]

The situation of white women and children on lonely ranches with their Chinese men servants, as described by Coolidge, was surely fraught with anxiety and laden with sexual imagery. During the nineteenth century, many among the white middle class believed that the lower classes were the repositories of sexual excess and depravity. Those households, accordingly, harbored fears that lower-class domestic servants would teach sexual deviance to the children under their care.[24] But asexual African American women—mammies—and feminized and asexual Chinese American men—houseboys—personified ideal domestic servants to white middle-class families because of their alleged ascriptions of race, gender, and sexuality. And yet, within the social lexicon of the nineteenth century, those apparently benign attributions, as inversions, carried malevolent gender and sexual meanings. Even as lascivious and sexually aggressive Asian women signaled manliness and lesbianism, passionless and sexually introverted Asian men signified womanliness and homosexuality.

The Chinese "bachelor societies" of the nineteenth century were surely racialized sites of sexual intemperance and abnormality. In that alien world of Chinatowns, thus, from a white viewpoint, all Chinese men were bachelors and all Chinese women were prostitutes. According to the newspaper, the *Marin Journal* of March 30, 1876, whites believed that a Chinese woman was "a prostitute from instinct, religion, education, and interest and degrading to all around her," and a Chinese man had "neither wife nor child, nor expects to have any."[25] Race, gender, and sexuality were thereby collapsed and conflated. Chinese "bachelor societies," along with the commonplace assertion of Chinese men's gender inversion, must have inspired notions of homosexuality and sexual deviance on the part of whites. In truth, the close and intimate associations of men in boarding houses in towns and bunkhouses in the rural districts and at lonely outposts of labor as in the mining camps afforded opportunities for homosexual relations among Chinese and Asian American men.[26] Whether directed by circumstances or by orientation, same-sex attractions and intimacies were likely present within nineteenth- and twentieth-century Chinese and Asian American men's culture, and in that way resembled some of the sexual relations among cowboys out on the range.[27]

Asian men and women's sexualities, however, were never static and took different turns within the white imagination, depending upon the social needs of the time. Chinese men might have been seen as passionless during the late nineteenth century, but they, like Japanese men, were reborn as predators of white women during the early twentieth century. Asia, according to many in the West, was wakened from centuries of dark slumber through the efforts of European peoples in trade, mission work, and colonial rule during the nineteenth century. That relationship, of course, was raced, gendered, and sexualized as theorized in that a white, energetic, and manly West stirred and aroused a nonwhite, recumbent, and womanly East. Tutored by whites, according to that version of history, Asians in the East and Asian migrants to the West learned science, technology, and industry and entered the modern world.

That entry, however, marked the rise of a counter to the West's originating deed—a raced, gendered, and sexualized threat, as imagined, to white global supremacy called the "yellow peril."

Perhaps coined by Germany's Kaiser Wilhelm II in 1895, the term "yellow peril" was illustrated in a painting he commissioned that positioned the nations of Europe—Austria, England, France, Germany, Italy, Russia, and "the smaller civilised States"—facing the alleged threat to their East. "Nations of Europe, defend your holiest possession," Wilhelm II had inscribed in the text to accompany the painting. Christianity and civilization, Europe's holiest possessions, were depicted as white women, the guardians of home and culture, and were threatened with destruction by heathenism and barbarism, represented by a buddha and a Chinese dragon.[28] Figuratively, thus, the "yellow peril" was the despoiling threat posed by Asian men or an aggressive heathenism and barbarism to European women or a pure Christianity and virtuous civilization.

In 1892, a decade after the passage of America's Chinese Exclusion Act, Denis Kearney, a labor and political leader in California, scored "the foreign Shylocks" in his anti-Semitic, anticapitalist rhetoric for "rushing another breed of Asiatic slaves to fill up the gap made vacant by the Chinese who are shut out by our laws. . . . Japs . . . are being brought here now in countless numbers to demoralize and discourage our domestic labor market and to be educated . . . at our expense." Kearney added, Japanese men "know no morals but vice" and sit in classrooms next to "our . . . daughters to debauch [and] demoralize them." Likewise, in 1909, Grove Johnson worried over his responsibility to "the mothers and fathers of Sacramento County who have their little daughters sitting side by side in the school rooms with matured Japs, with their base minds, their lascivious thoughts, multiplied by their race and strengthened by their mode of life. . . . I have seen Japanese twenty-five years old," Johnson declared, "sitting in the seats next to the pure maids of California. . . . I shudder . . . to think of such a condition."[29] A white woman warned that Japanese men were "casting furtive glances at our young women," and a California newspaper alleged in 1920 that "Japanese boys are taught by their elders to look upon . . . American girls with a view to future sex relations. . . ."[30] Seduction and rape, according to those narratives, were the designs of adult Japanese men for white female schoolchildren. Although considered a conquest, the imagined acts attested not to Japanese men's masculinity, but, like Chinese men, exemplified an aberrant and diminished sexual capacity, this ravishment of white girls.

Miscegenation was another aspect of the of the "yellow peril," sexual threat a voluntary but misguided crossing over of white women to nonwhite men. "Near my home is an eighty-acre tract of as fine land as there is in California," began Ralph Newman, a former Congregational clergyman. "On that tract lives a Japanese. With that Japanese lives a white woman. In that woman's arms is a baby. What is that baby? It isn't a Japanese. It isn't white. It is a germ of the mightiest problem that ever faced this state; a problem that will make the black problem of the South look white."[31] Newman's hyperbole appeared ludicrous because of the small number of Japanese men in California and an even smaller number who cohabited with or married white women. However, his concern involved not numbers, but a principle and a breach in the wall of racial "purity" and sexual privilege. That biracial baby, the offspring of the union between a white woman and a nonwhite man, testified to the falsity of the claim that a precise, unbridgeable line divided white from nonwhite, and exemplified an erosion of the exclusive privilege claimed by white men over white women. That was Newman's "mightiest problem."

In 1915, about two years after the telling of Newman's remarkable tale, Cecil B. DeMille's movie *The Cheat* was shown to captivated audiences. The movie told the sorry story of a white socialite whose extravagance led her to strike a bargain with a Japanese merchant for cash in exchange for sex. Edith, played by Fannie Ward, is branded and thereby symbolically violated and raped by the Asian man, played by Sessue Hayakawa, when she refuses to consummate the deal. Instead, she shoots her assailant and is taken to court. During the trial, her husband assumes blame for the shooting. Deeply bothered by her complicity and her husband's gallantry and false conviction, Edith rushes up to the bench, pulls down her dress, and brushes back her blond hair

Fig. 11. Scene from Cecil B. DeMille's movie *The Cheat* (1915).
The elegantly dressed Tori (Sessue Hayakawa) moves seamlessly between the white world of high society and the nonwhite realm of criminality and sensuality as he offers Edith (Fannie Ward) the choice of sex or an embarrassing public undressing. Image courtesy of the Wisconsin Center for Film Research.

to reveal the cruel brand on her pale, bare shoulder. The white men in the courtroom erupt in anger, but the "lynch mob" is quieted and a cheer of relief goes up when the judge sets aside the guilty verdict. Film critics reported that the movie's viewers felt a closeness to the white protagonists. "One of the men that sat behind me in the Strand Theatre said, 'I would like to be in that mob,' " wrote a reviewer.[32] Even as it affirmed white patriarchy, *The Cheat* warned against women's independence with the threat of rape by nonwhite men. Edith's pollution was forgiven by her husband's sacrifice and the judge's final verdict, and it was displaced onto the Japanese villain whose manliness derived from the bulge in his wallet and not his pants. Edith had promised him sex only because she lusted for his cash. The courtroom's lynch mob, finally, admonished nonwhite men to stay on their side of the racial divide, because white men would resort to both legal and extralegal means to preserve their exclusive control over white women.

Asian men, it seemed, bore generalizing attributes that transferred from one ethnic group to another. Thus, when *The Cheat* was released again in 1918, the Japanese villain became a Burmese man, because Japan and America were allies during World War I. And the role of Japanese or Chinese men who preyed upon white women in the early twentieth century easily included Filipino men during the 1920s and 1930s. Besides the resources of money or political power that Asian men allegedly deployed to seduce white women, they were also accused of flashing their good looks and clothes to lure white women to their downfall. A writer observed in 1913 that when Japanese men dressed in "up-to-date suits and possibly patent leather shoes, they at once are said to be 'cocky.' "[33] Similarly, Judge D. W. Rohrback of California's Monterey County called Filipinos "little brown men attired like 'Solomon in all his glory,' strutting like peacocks and endeavoring to attract the eyes of young American and Mexican girls."[34] And less kindly, C. M. Goethe, president of the Immigration Study Commission, declared in 1931: "The Filipino tends to interbreed with near-moron white girls. The resulting hybrid is almost invariably undesirable. The ever increasing brood of children of Filipino coolie fathers and low-grade white mothers may in time constitute a serious social burden."[35] Goethe's claim resonated with the tenets of eugenics, a contemporary science that had fallen into disrepute among most scientists by the 1930s, but had maintained a sure grip upon the public imagination. It proposed that sexual promiscuity, immorality, sexual deviance, and feeblemindedness were all genetically determined and linked.[36] Genetic explanations for supposed racial or bodily and behavioral or cultural differences would persist over the years, despite much evidence to the contrary, and racializations would continue to be coupled with sexualizations.[37]

Of course, we must recognize that Asian (and African and European) women and men know that representations of them created by others, whether by writers, politicians, or scientists, are not necessarily consonant with reality or with how they think about themselves. The alleged sexualities of Asians are a case in point. Despite the commonly believed attributions of them as inversions—feminized men or masculinized women—or as homosexuals or deviant heterosexuals, as hyper- or hypo-sexualized, Asian Americans knew better. So although a University of California professor, David P. Barrows, might declare in 1931 that Filipino vices "are almost entirely based on sexual passion" and that without a "wholesome society of his own," he [the Filipino] would spend "the residue of his savings in brothels and dancehalls," Filipino Americans like Manuel Buaken could offer eloquent testaments to their basic humanity. "I was wounded deeply in heart and soul for on that day I had tasted more pangs of life's bitterness and all the sordidness of this world than I [had] ever known before," Buaken wrote of his encounters with racism in America in 1948, "and I learned what calamity and what tragic consequences race prejudice can inflict upon a man's life."[38] And although he played the part of villainous Asian men in numerous films, the Asian American actor Sessue Hayakawa noted: "Such roles are not true to our Japanese nature. . . . They are fake and give people the wrong idea of us. I wish to make a characterization which shall reveal us as we really are."[39]

And yet, despite their core hollowness, representations wield undeniable power. They frame the possibilities within which we, each of us, must operate. We can contest or we can acquiesce to the limits they impose. But they determine in large measure the course and consequences of our choices. And they accrue legitimacy, whether ordained by God or nature, by assuming the mantle of religion or science and the common sense of everyday speech. As the anthropologist Marshall Sahlins pointed out, sexual reproduction and intercourse appear "*a priori* as a biological fact, characterized as an urge of human nature independent of the relations between social persons . . . [and] acting *upon* society from without (or below)." Yet, Sahlins urges, we must conceive of both "the act and the partners as socially defined and contemplated . . . according to a symbolic code of persons, practices and proprieties."[40] In other words, sexuality (and I might add geographies, race, and gender) and the persons and categories of heterosexual and homosexual (and West and East, white and black, man and woman) are social constructions that serve particular purposes and functions for specific relations, societies, and times.

"Ever since the seventeenth century," according to historians D'Emilio and Freedman, "European migrants to America had merged racial and sexual ideology in order to differentiate themselves from Indians and blacks, to strengthen the mechanisms of social control over slaves, and to justify the appropriation of Indian and Mexican lands through the destruction of native peoples and their cultures."[41] That need to differentiate gained new urgency during the nineteenth century when conflicts between the industrial machine and agricultural garden, West and East, white and nonwhite, man and woman, citizen and alien, capitalist and worker, increased and intensified. Scientific and popular thought supported the idea of white supremacy, a cord that helped hold together a fractured and fracturing nation, and white women's sexual purity was purchased by nonwhite women's supposed immorality and by laws and practices that punished interracial unions. Simultaneously, white men exempted themselves from those prohibitions, authorizing themselves free sexual access to nonwhite women, and therewith flexed their powers and rights of conquest in an age of westward expansion and overseas empire over white women and nonwhite women and men.

To explain their privileges, whites reinscribed and benefited from the dualisms of geographies (West and East) and race (white and black), of white men, gender (man and woman), and white heterosexual men, and of sexuality (heterosexual and homosexual) that formed hierarchies and correspondences between and among them. Those structures, we must remember, are mere facades, like Chicago's White City and the Midway Plaisance, which were erected to convey certain notions about humans and their societies, but were torn down and reduced to rubble after they had served their purposes. They are creations; they are not preordained; they are not permanent. Still, although fictional and fleeting, they substantially comprise the reality of our identities and interactions. They are thus made real through our acceptance or rejection of them and our acting upon or against them. We experience, in the active and passive senses, their powers. Within that realm, the West and whiteness form a cluster with manliness and heterosexuality; and the East and nonwhiteness, with womanliness and homosexuality or deviant heterosexuality. Those clusters in turn are ordered vertically in such a way that the former is deemed to be superior, the latter, inferior; the former constitutes the norm, the latter, a deviation from the norm; the former is rendered citizen, the latter, alien.

Despite their ability to name and therewith authorize, dualisms and their very necessity reveal the existence of transgressions against the ruling regimes. Their hold is tenuous. Think of it this way; from one point of view, the creation of categories such as geographies, race, gender, and sexuality, their enforcement through cultural maps, ideas, institutions, and practices, and their punishment of deviations from those norms that might include fines, imprisonment, and lynching exemplify an overwhelming power that could easily be taken for granted and accepted as natural and immutable. But from another vantage point, those implements of control are required because people believe and behave contrary to those strictures of separation between West and East, white and nonwhite, man and woman, heterosexual and homosexual. Laws that forbade sexual relations between white and nonwhite or between man and man and woman and woman were passed because people engaged in those practices.

And the marshalling of science about the turn of the century marked a profound anxiety among the ruling class over the maintenance of social order amidst fractures and violations of geographies, race, gender, and sexuality. Through expansion, immigration, and industrialization, America had become even more racially diverse, women challenged men's dominance, and sexual minorities formed vibrant subcultures. The established domains were in flux and their outcomes uncertain. Upon self-reflection, that lesson of history, that social categories can be made and unmade, bespeaks an obvious truth. In the end, we

Fig. 12. A Wedding in the Chinese Quarter—Mott Street, New York (1890).

Ostensibly a representation of the Chinese wedding party in the background, a Chinese man bowed from labor and an interracial couple and their biracial offspring foreground the drawing. Miscegenation and reproduction were clearly apprehensions of the time for those intent on preserving "whiteness" and racial "purity," and the children playing on the curb might have hinted at a more amicable future for interracial relations or a foreboding of continued miscegenation. *Harper's Weekly*, November 22, 1890, 908–909, courtesy of HarpWeek LLC.

know that within us all there are elements of both presumed poles of East and West, black and white, woman and man, homosexual and heterosexual, and their attributions. The lines that are said to divide them are truly smudges that blur and merge one with the other.

As represented during the late nineteenth century, Asian bodies—raced, gendered, sexualized—both affirmed and denied the dualism of heterosexual and homosexual and its assumed naturalism and hierarchy. Biology, the argument proposed, determined those distinctions and values that applied to sexuality, but also, insofar as they were linked one to another, determined gender and in turn race, comprising a Victorian race/gender/sexuality system that in part explained and structured people's lives and relations. Asian inferiority as nonwhites who were "half-devil and half-child," as lewd women and diminutive men, as homosexuals and deviant heterosexuals, advanced white superiority as the normative, the exemplar of race, gender, and sexuality. But even as science sought to define homosexuals as a class of persons with certain traits, deviations from the norm pointed to the reality that the boundary between heterosexual and homosexual was fluid and impossible to demarcate definitively. And imagined differences, deployed to validate whiteness, manliness, and heterosexuality, provoked repulsion but also whetted desires and, at the least, curiosity. Perversions arouse our interest, because they threaten to rend the social fabric and at the same time extend the range and diversity of the goods available in the supermarket of race, gender, and sexuality. What really went down, we might ask with trepidation and loathing and with wonder and longing, at the Persian Palace of Eros?

CHAPTER 5

American History

"Determine if the prisoner, in addition to his masculine organs, has external female organs. If he does not, determine whether he might have had female organs in the past," ordered the French court in 1986 in the case of Bernard Boursicot and Shi Pei Pu, the former a French spy accused of supplying intelligence to the Chinese government through his lover, Shi, whom he believed to have been a woman. "Determine whether the prisoner shows any trace of surgical intervention of the sexual organs. If so, make a report of the nature of that intervention. Determine whether the prisoner, as he has claimed, has the ability to withdraw his penis and testicles into his body cavity. Examine the prisoner's anus for signs of sodomization."[1]

The indeterminacy of the imagined Asian body—its race, gender, sexuality—might have created anxieties among some non-Asians, but surely not among most Asians themselves. The case of the French spy and the Chinese counterspy exemplified, perhaps, how images can shape a person's perceptions and how another might use those illusions to stage magic, as in Oz, a circus, or a freak show. We see, oftentimes, what we want to see. Boursicot arrived in China in 1964 as an accountant for the French Embassy in Beijing.[2] At an embassy party, he met a young man, Shi, who was a writer of operas and plays, he said, and taught Chinese to the children of a French Embassy official. Boursicot and Shi soon became great friends, the former entranced by Chinese culture and the stories the latter told him, from Chinese history, of emperors, empresses, and court intrigues. One day, on a walk through the palaces and courtyards of the Forbidden City, Shi whispered to his friend that he was, in truth, a woman disguised as a man, the converse of Chinese operas in which men often played the roles of women. Boursicot believed Shi because he wanted to, and his attraction for his Chinese friend, formerly deviant as homosexuality, now became normalized as heterosexual desire. Boursicot dreamed of making love to Shi.

Boursicot pressed Shi. Shi replied, "Not now." A few weeks later, in June 1965, they agreed on a date for their first sexual encounter. Shi arrived at Boursicot's apartment at six o'clock. They embraced, Boursicot gently kissed Shi's neck and began to undress her. Shi demurred and offered to undress herself. She took off her manly clothes down to her undergarments. Boursicot trembled, perhaps because he had never before had sex with a woman. He went into the bathroom to put on a condom. He returned, they had sex, and, as Boursicot would later recall, it was not as erotic or satisfying as he had imagined. Shortly before Boursicot was scheduled to leave China at the end of that year, Shi told him that she suspected that she was pregnant. Boursicot left China promising to return. But Boursicot was away for four years, and when he returned as an archivist for the French Embassy, he had with him an address that was two years old.

Somehow Boursicot managed to find Shi, who informed him that they had a son, although the boy was being hidden because of the current hatred of foreigners. In fact, she warned him, they were being watched, and indeed the police broke into Shi's home one day, took her away, and questioned Boursicot. Despite the danger, the couple maintained a clandestine relationship at first, but later, after Boursicot had agreed to supply the Chinese government with files copied from his work as embassy archivist, he and Shi were allowed to see each other more often, although they were lucky to have sex twice a month. Still, Boursicot loved Shi, and thought about getting her and their son out of China. He petitioned his Chinese contacts to allow that, but they refused. In 1972, Boursicot's second embassy tour ended, and he returned to France. Over the years, Boursicot realized that he was bisexual and had affairs with both men and women. Eventually, in 1982, Shi and Bertrand, their son, arrived in Paris to share Boursicot's apartment with him and his male lover.

French intelligence found interesting that arrangement of a civil servant and a Chinese national living together in Paris. On the morning of June 30, 1983, security agents brought Boursicot in for questioning, and two days later they charged him with espionage. They interviewed Shi on July 1 and, based on the testimony provided by Boursicot, they noted in their files: "Shi Pei Pu was raised right from the start, as a boy by her mother. Her true nature was hidden from everyone until this day."[3] That identity, nonetheless, was questioned by a judge, who ordered the medical examination that determined that Shi was, in truth, a man physically. Further, blood tests revealed that Bertrand was not the son of either Boursicot or Shi. To the judge's reprimand that he had lied, Shi reportedly replied: "I thought France was a democratic country. Is it important if I am a man or a woman?" And as if to demonstrate his gender and sexual ambiguity during the medical examination, Shi, according to a reporter, pushed his testicles up into his body cavity and pulled his penis back between his legs to bisect his dangling scrotal sac. "The penis is hidden, while the skin of the scrotum resembles the vaginal lips, beneath a triangle of pubic hair," the reporter surmised. "Pushed between the empty scrotal sac, the penis has also created a small cavity so that shallow penetration is possible." But, the reporter concluded, Shi's unusual physical ability was insufficient as an explanation for the befuddlement of a man versed in various sexual practices such as this Frenchman, Boursicot, over the course of twenty years. "It was only an illusion," the reporter noted of Shi's performance. "But 90 percent of love, even a man of science will volunteer, is illusion. In defense of love, a story we love, a person we love, is there anyone among us who has not closed his eyes and refused to see?"[4]

The story inspired not only laughter and locker-room jokes among men confident in their sexual abilities to recognize a woman when they saw one, but also a serious, Tony award–winning play in 1988 by an Asian American writer, David Henry Hwang, entitled *M. Butterfly.* The author's choice of title is more than fortuitous, conjuring the images portrayed in Giacomo Puccini's well-known classic opera *Madama Butterfly* that debuted at La Scala in 1904. The story tells the tale of Benjamin Franklin Pinkerton, an American naval officer stationed in Japan at the turn of the century, and his fifteen-year-old bride, the geisha

Cho-Cho-San, or "butterfly" in Japanese. Pinkerton is a "vagabond Yankee" who plucks "the flowers of every region," while Cho-Cho-San is sedentary to Japan and virginal because of her youth, but simultaneously sexually knowledgeable because of her profession, that of a geisha whose very employment and sole purpose was to ensure men's pleasure. Pinkerton impregnates Cho-Cho-San, abandons her, marries a white American, and returns to Japan to reclaim his son. When Cho-Cho-San discovers her husband's new and parallel life, she commits suicide by stabbing herself with a knife.[5]

The opera's tropes are all very familiar. Geography is represented by the proverbial, antithetical East and West, such that they remain forever apart. Pinkerton is mobile and returns home to the United States, where he settles down to a normal American life; Cho-Cho-San is stationary and ostracized by her people for her marriage and her abandonment of Japanese men and culture. Race forms a gulf, an unbridgeable distance between white and nonwhite, and the race mixture results in a tragic, foreign issue. The Japanese, the opera tells us, were silent and humble and accustomed to little things. Gender and men's dominance over women are idealized in the supposed role of the geisha who served men and in the figure of Cho-Cho-San who remains faithful to and sacrifices herself for her husband. Sexuality appears in Pinkerton's unbridled, healthy heterosexuality and in Cho-Cho-San's perversity as both virgin and whore. Even in dying, Cho-Cho-San penetrates herself autoerotically with a phallic knife. Those binaries of geographies, race, gender, and sexuality in Puccini's opera are clearly demarcated, remain fixed, and attempts to cross them are doomed to failure.

For David Henry Hwang, the real-life situation of Bernard Boursicot and Shi Pei Pu provided an opportunity for a play that worked to subvert those conventions in *Madama Butterfly*. "It all started in May of 1986, over casual dinner conversation," Hwang recalled. "A friend asked, had I heard about the French diplomat who'd fallen in love with a Chinese actress, who subsequently turned out to be not only a spy, but a man?" From the brief two-paragraph story in the *New York Times*, Hwang concluded that "the diplomat must have fallen in love, not with a person, but with a fantasy stereotype," and that "to the extent the Chinese spy encouraged these misperceptions, he must have played up to and exploited the image of the Oriental woman as demure and submissive. . . . I suspected there was a play here." Asian women, Hwang knew, were not all demure and submissive. It occurred to him that the story seemed an inversion of the Puccini opera, where instead of "yet another lotus blossom pining away for a cruel Caucasian man, and dying for her love," the Asian man fools the fantasy-driven Frenchman.[6]

And so it is that in the play we find the Frenchman, an ex-diplomat named René Gallimard, in prison—a literal prison for his crime, but also a symbolic prison of his own creation. "Butterfly, Butterfly," Gallimard pines in the play's opening line. "The limits of my cell are as such: four-and-a-half meters by five. . . . It's an enchanted space I occupy," he declares of his prison cell.[7] Gallimard, explained anthropologist Dorinne K. Kondo, had created "a space of fantasy, a prison of cultural conventions and stereotypes" that had captured and imprisoned him and made him "the willing sacrificial victim of his own culturally and historically produced conventions" of geography, race, and gender.[8] The play's story line has Gallimard seduced by an opera star, Song Liling, who first wins the Frenchman's affection with her/his performance of the death scene from *Madama Butterfly* at a party in the home of the German ambassador in Beijing. In subsequent encounters, Song enchants Gallimard with orientalist tropes and trappings of an unchanging Chinese culture and tradition, of women's modesty and submissiveness, of the promise of fantastic sexual delights. Gallimard falls madly in love, passes on intelligence secrets to this Chinese spy, and even after having been confronted with the physical reality of Song's "manhood," confesses to "choose fantasy." "There is a vision of the Orient that I have," he persists. "Of slender women in chong sams and kimonos who die for the love of unworthy foreign devils. Who are born and raised to be the perfect women." In the end, Gallimard becomes Butterfly, assumes her form, and commits suicide with the words: "Yes—love. Why not admit it all. That was my undoing, wasn't it? Love warped my judgment, blinded my eyes, rearranged the very lines on my face . . . until I could look in the mirror and see nothing but . . . a woman."[9]

Throughout Gallimard's fixation and transformation, Song tries to disabuse him of his simpleminded notions of East and West, white and nonwhite, man and woman, straight and gay. "Consider it this way: what would you say if a blonde homecoming queen fell in love with a short Japanese businessman?" Song asked Gallimard in reversing the plot of *Madama Butterfly*. "He treats her cruelly, then goes home for three years, during which time she prays to his picture and turns down marriage from a young Kennedy. Then, when she learns he has remarried, she kills herself. Now, I believe you would consider this girl to be a deranged idiot, correct? But because it's an Oriental who kills herself for a Westerner—ah!—you find it beautiful."[10] And after disrobing and revealing his genitals to Gallimard, Song protests that he is not "just a man," in the Frenchman's words; he can dance "like a woman," his skin is sumptuously soft "like a woman," the curve of his face and touch of his hair are like those of "a woman." "I'm your Butterfly," Song teases Gallimard. "Under the robes, beneath everything, it was always me."[11] The categories of man and woman, Song explains, are creations of our imagination, of our closed eyes. That a man can play a woman, allegedly even better than a woman can play herself, as in a Chinese opera, exemplifies the assumed power of men over women and the power of images that are mere conjurings but that serve to define the identities we ascribe to others. Beneath the robes, the outward guises we assume and project onto others, resides the true self, the "always me." Through inversions, *M. Butterfly* highlights the artifice of social categories and the truth of their underlying complexities, where binaries alone cannot account for the crossovers and diversities that abound such that there is neither East nor West, white nor nonwhite, man nor woman, straight nor gay. Before his death scene, Gallimard transforms himself into a geisha by painting his face and putting on a wig and kimono. He thereby embodies at the last East and West, white and nonwhite, man and woman, and normative and deviant sexualities as he plunges the knife into himself. Of his final discovery, Gallimard exults: "It is 19__. And I have found her [Butterfly] at last. In a prison on the outskirts of Paris. My name is René Gallimard—also known as Madame Butterfly."[12]

Binaries, in truth, are simplistic. They surely do not capture the entirety of human experience. And yet they seem to persist, over decades, over centuries, from one culture and society to another. They are at once familiar and foreign. And their very resilience suggests their problematic. Binaries require repetition in different times and places—require repackaging to suit changing contexts and conditions as they are challenged, altered, and even rejected. In 1917, British author Thomas Burke published *Limehouse Nights*, a collection of short stories that reinscribed many of the prevailing binaries. Burke was a contemporary and admirer of American writer Ambrose Bierce, who, in his story "The Haunted Valley," had presented the reader with the ambiguities of race, gender, and sexuality in the characters of Jo. Dunfer and Ah Wee. "All I had was perhaps a desire to emulate—to tell a story as ably as Ambrose Bierce and to see and write as clearly as Stephen Crane," Burke explained of his ambition. *Limehouse Nights* made Burke's reputation as a writer of short stories, and was hailed by London's critics as "a work of genius" and as comprising "masterpieces."[13] The first story in the book, entitled "The Chink and the Child," was the best known of those "masterpieces" largely because American film director D. W. Griffith's classic movie, *Broken Blossoms*, was based upon it. But the story also gained notoriety on its own (Burke and his publisher feared that the book would be censored), because "The Chink and the Child" told a tale of miscegenation.

"The Chink and the Child," recalled Burke, grew from "a little incident witnessed in the market place at Aylesbury." What that incident was is unclear, but the story's conception was consistent with Burke's writing style. Burke knew London intimately, and many of his stories derived from his walks and observations about the city. The subject matter, however, London's Chinese, was completely unfamiliar to Burke. "At the time I had no knowledge of the Chinese people," he admitted, "and all I knew

of Limehouse and the district was what I had automatically observed without any aim or purpose during my unguided wan-
derings in remote London. I had thus been able to write those
stories with the peculiar assurance of a man who knows nothing
of what he is writing or talking about."[14] But Burke's conventions, his orientalisms, could not have materialized from the vac-
uum of a writer "who knows nothing of what he is writing or
talking about." Burke's recuperation of British orientalisms was
steeped within particular traditions of time and place,[15] and it
repeated and reconstituted an aesthetic and a formula that conse-
quently resonated with peculiar clarity and force among his
readers.

Asians—the Chinese—in my reading of Burke, are positioned
within the liminal space of empire and metropole, overseas and
Britain, foreign and domestic, and East and West, and Asian bodies are similarly situated along the borderlands of race, gender,
and sexual differences. The terrain is simultaneously ambiguous
and contested, familiar and queer, and hence fraught with fear
and hatred, affection and attraction. "It is a tale of love and lovers that they tell in the low-lit Causeway that slinks from West
India Dock Road to the dark waste of waters beyond," begins
Burke's tale of binaries—"the Chink" and "the child." Limehouse, that "low-lit Causeway" and site of perversity and pleasure, together with its denizens of homegrown outcasts and immigrants—the residues of empire—"slinks" from self's
gateway—"the portals of the West"—to and from "the dark
waste of waters beyond."[16]

Like Limehouse, the story's protagonist—the child, Lucy—is
pinned between two contending forces: her father, Battling Bur-
rows, and her lover, Cheng Huan, the chink, the yellow man.
Battling epitomized masculinity as a boxer, "the lightning wel-
terweight of Shadwell," and was fond of "wine, woman and
song," surely all manly sports.[17] Cheng exemplified femininity as
a loafer and poet, "he felt things more passionately," and lived
all alone watching the street, the marketplace, from the interior
spaces of his home. And like Pierre Loti's "artificial and light"
Japanese women, Cheng was an inversion, fleeting and without

substance; he was "like a figure of a shadowgraph." He was a man, but also a woman. Battling, too, was an aberration, "a curious mixture of athleticism and degeneracy," masculinity gone wild in his excesses of drinking, womanizing, and beating (and perhaps sexually abusing) his daughter Lucy. He was thus "a type that upsets all accepted classifications"—a deviant member of the white race, a sexual pervert, and a "sensualist," a man/woman ruled by his emotions, his body and not his mind.[18]

Lucy, illegitimate and "a little girl of twelve," is further positioned in an equivocal space at the juncture of a sexual coming of age, between child and woman, a blossom about to be broken.[19] Lucy's beauty, "the toss of the head and the hang of the little blue skirt as it coyly kissed her knee," wrote Burke of her symbolic deflowering, smote Cheng and "the spirit of poetry broke her blossoms all about his odorous chamber." Her abuse formed a basis of Burke's pornography. "Yet, for all the starved face and the transfixed air," wrote the novelist of Lucy suggestively, "there was a lurking beauty about her, a something that called you in the soft curve of her cheek that cried for kisses and was fed with blows, and in the splendid mournfulness that grew in eyes and lips. The brown hair chimed against the pale face, like the rounding of a verse." Her tattered dress could not hide "the loveliness of her slender figure or the shy grace of her movements." The binary of manliness and womanliness, of sadism and masochism—the association of inflicting pain to achieve sexual pleasure—cheeks that "cried for kisses" but were "fed with blows," and Lucy's "splendid mournfulness" must have titillated some of Burke's readers.[20]

After a particularly brutal beating and expulsion from her home, Lucy found her way to a bagnio, a brothel and "Oriental slave pen," where Cheng spotted her with "his intent gaze" and saved her from "horrors" that "cannot be told" (just simply fantasized). "What he brought to her," wrote Burke of Cheng's rescue, in language steeped in Freudian dualism, "was love and death." He led her to his room: "Slowly, softly they mounted the stairs to his room," where he "crooned over her," kissed her hands, "her cheek and lip and little bosom," removed her "besmirched rags," and covered her with robes and showered her with gifts from the empire, "strange things . . . formless masses of blue and gold, magical things of silk, and a vessel that was surely Aladdin's lamp, and a box of spices." Thus, made over and adorned, Lucy, the "alabaster Cockney child," the "white perfection," was transformed by Cheng into "a Chinese lyric." Those two days of domestic bliss, of tending "as might mother to child" (and as an asexual Chinese domestic manservant might have nursed a white woman and her children on a lonely farm in the American West) were shattered by an angry and indignant Battling, who learned of his child's crossover to yellow men: "Of all the creeping things that creep upon the earth the most insidious is the Oriental in the West," Battling believed.[21] He found and retrieved Lucy during Cheng's absence, and repatriated her to his domain.

Burke's "Oriental in the West" surely evoked Limehouse and the yellow peril, and the "Oriental slave pen" as described by Burke recalled uncannily the Midway Plaisance's Persian Palace of Eros. The room, he wrote, was bathed in "a purple dusk" with a few lanterns that "stung the glooms." "Low couches lay around the walls, and strange men decorated them: Chinese, Japs, Malays, Lascars, with one or two white girls; and sleek, noiseless attendants swam from couch to couch." In a far corner, a sprawled figure clutched the stem of a spent pipe, and lounging together were "a scorbutic nigger" and "a Jewess from Shadwell." "Squatting on a table in the centre, beneath one of the lanterns, was a musician with a reed, blinking upon the company like a sly cat, and making his melody of six repeated notes." The place stank. "The atmosphere churned," was Burke's choice description. "The dirt of years, tobacco of many growings, opium, betel nut, and moist flesh allied themselves in one grand assault against the nostrils." There, into that putrid den of iniquity, that lair of "the Oriental in the West," had come Lucy, Cheng's prey and "snowy-breasted pearl."[22]

Horrified with Lucy's abduction, a frantic Cheng rushed over to Battling's house and there found in the darkness Lucy's broken body, described erotically by Burke: "A few rags of clothing were

Fig. 13. Scene from D. W. Griffith's movie *Broken Blossoms* (1919).
"So, in the ghastly Limehouse morning," wrote Burke, "they found—the dead child, and the Chink, kneeling beside her, with a sharp knife gripped in a vice-like hand, its blade far between his ribs." Quotation from Thomas Burke, "Chink and the Child," in *Limehouse Nights* (London: Grosset & Dunlap, 1917), 35–36. Image courtesy of the Wisconsin Center for Film and Theatre Research.

about her pale, slim body; her hair hung limp as her limbs; her eyes were closed." The yellow man reclaimed the child's body covered with whip marks and welts—marked by sex and death, bearing the inscriptions of the poet from the East and the boxer from the West—carried it to his room, and covered it with "blue and yellow silks," before plunging a sharp knife "far between his ribs." Cheng's penetration was, like Cho-Cho-San's in *Madama Butterfly*, autoerotic. Battling met a similar fate that night, when Cheng's "love-gift," a serpent and another phallic symbol, that he had left on the boxer's couch bit, injected its venom, and strangled the drunken "Tetrarch of the ring." Cheng's revenge was gendered and sexual, but was administered by a surrogate, a more potent masculine organ than his own.

Death was the only resolution for those who occupied the margins of space, race, gender, sexuality, age, and civility—Cheng, Battling, and Lucy—but only Cheng's demise was self-inflicted because for him, wrote Burke, like a servant without a master, a Chinese domestic without his child-keep, "Life was no longer possible; and life without his little lady, his White Blossom, was no longer desirable."[23] As natives of Limehouse, Cheng, Battling, and Lucy were squatters on the frontier between light and darkness, civilization and barbarism, middle-class sensibility and working-class senselessness, hygiene and filth, normality and deformity. Their bodies, moreover, were marked by their borderland habitat—Cheng's migration from East to West and his flirtations with miscegenation, together with the indeterminateness and inversions of his race, gender, and sexuality; Battling's crossovers of race, gender, and sexuality as a white man/woman and sadist; and Lucy's suspension between East and West, Cheng and Battling, childhood and adulthood, asexuality and sexuality, and her masochism and racial crossover to yellow men. All of those transgressions threatened to breach the moats and embankments of civilization and its categories and the binaries that constitute them—inclusive of geographies, race, gender, and sexuality. Burke's trio were metaphoric border crossers, illegal immigrants who had to be tracked, captured, and expelled from the civil state. Like White City's sanitation system, for the sake of order, for purity, for wellness, there could be no tolerance for refuse, and the demise of the fugitives and their removal were their inevitable and logical outcomes and destinations.

Binaries resist change, perhaps, because they offer coherence especially during times of social upheaval and disorganization. They present us with explanations for social structures—geographies, race, gender, sexuality—and their relations, and they supply us with justifications for shoring them up against any threatening tide. They offer us quick fixes, as a means by which to make and preserve rule amidst apparent chaos.[24] A case in point is the late nineteenth century—a period of great anxiety and stress and simultaneously an era of fervent reconstruction. The continental frontier's end, an influx of "new" immigrants, and racial and class conflict motivated a nationalism that fantasized an exceptional and homogeneous white West and white Republic. Space, especially coastal, urban space, wherein surged aliens and immigrants, and the postbellum South, from whence emanated an exodus of the newly freed, demanded containment and coercion, as undertaken in White City's architecture of monumental buildings and broad avenues, its omnipresent police force, and its separation from and contrast with the Midway Plaisance. A science of race that named and ordered human types and cultures arose and thrived amidst racial and ethnic diversity, the results of immigration, but also of overseas expansion. Racist and restrictive immigration and segregation laws and practices sought to end border crossings and to annul racial and ethnic impulses for inclusion and equality. A white middle-class women's movement for opportunities in education, employment, and politics was countered by a white middle-class men's ideology of the differently constituted and the cult of manliness. And a science and politics of sexuality that defined and regulated homosexuals and sexual deviance emerged from apprehensions over thriving gay male subcultures and changes in the sexualized racial and gender formations.

The same can be said about the late twentieth century, which, like the late nineteenth century, was an era of renewed immigration and diversity sparked by the 1965 Immigration Act, which ended racial discrimination in the entry of peoples, and by higher birth rates among nonwhites than among whites. Those new Americans, comprising mainly Latinos and Asians, built new communities in urban centers from the East to West coasts, but also in small towns, in the interiors, and in the South and Southwest. The magnitude of those demographic changes was mirrored in the percentage increase in population from 1980 to 1990. During that decade, whites grew by 4.3 percent nationally, African Americans by 13 percent, Latinos by 49.8 percent, and Asians by 93.9 percent. And as the numerical gap between

Fig. 14. "The Problem Solved" (c.1870s).

The problem of the late nineteenth century, this poster shows, was immigrants and the threat they posed for the U.S. Here, an Irish man from the East and a Chinese man in womanly dress and an erect queue from the West devour a stiff Uncle Sam. The erection reaches new heights with the final swallowing. Spatial, racial, gendered, and sexual images abound in this representation of the period's "great fear." Courtesy of the Wong Ching Foo Collection.

whites and nonwhites closed, the ethnic diversity of America's peoples widened. Asian migrants, for instance, came to the United States not only from Asia but also from Africa, Latin America, and Europe, to which they had migrated first, and they included East Asians (Chinese, Koreans, Japanese) and Southeast Asians, South Asians, and West Asians (from Filipinos and Vietnamese, to Indians and Pakistanis, to Iranis and Iraqis), along with an array of languages, foods, and religions.

The United States and world economies underwent transformation from industrialism to postindustrialism, from local to global markets and networks, and from old to new centers of production and wealth. Capital, labor, goods, information, and culture moved swiftly in complicated flows within and across nation-states; and multiplicities and hybridities, flux and doubt undermined notions of insularity, stability, and permanence. Conflicts over the meanings and relations of geographies, race, gender, sexuality, class, and citizenship heightened with the stakes, and they acquired the expressions of armed conflicts and calamities of epic proportions—culture wars, a clash of civilizations, national disasters, and wars.[25] Political boundaries and alliances were created and redrawn, and racial, ethnic, gender, sexual, and religious nationalisms and fundamentalisms both within and without the United States found deep and fertile soil in the anxieties of the age. Binaries—West and East, white and black, man and woman, heterosexual and homosexual—flourished under those reactionary regimes, albeit modified and spruced up for the occasion. It was as if some yearned for a return to the imagined simplicity and sureties of Kansas.

In 1982, one hundred years after a law barred the entry of Chinese workers into the United States because, the Exclusion Act declared, they endangered the domestic tranquility, a Chinese American was beaten to death by two white men, autoworkers in Detroit, because they allegedly said that he was a "Jap" and "It's because of you motherfuckers that we're out of work." The fatal encounter began in the sexually charged atmosphere of a topless bar, and it continued outside where one of Vincent Chin's assailants held him while the other clubbed his head, chest, and knees with a baseball bat. Chin, the only son of Lily and Hing Chin, was a draftsman whose father was a veteran of World War II and whose mother's great-grandfather was a railroad laborer in nineteenth-century America. "I don't understand how this could happen in America," his mother cried. "My husband fought for this country. We always paid our taxes and worked hard. Before, I really loved America, but now this has made me very angry." Chin's assailants pleaded guilty to manslaughter and received sentences of three years' probation and a fine of

$3000 and $780 in fees. "Three thousand dollars can't even buy a good used car these days," lamented a Chinese American, "and this was the price of a life."[26]

Times change, circumstances differ, but the desire to systematize, organize, and sort by similarities and differences, to arrange in oppositional binarics that order, explain, and sanitize, endures. Three years after Chin's death, J. Philippe Rushton of Canada's University of Western Ontario's psychology department posited his "differential K theory" to organize and explain what he perceived to be individual and group differences, including life histories, social behavior, and physiological functioning. "K" refers to one end of a continuum of reproductive strategies characterized by the production of very few offspring with a heavy investment in the rearing of each as evidenced in mammals, while "r" refers to the other end, typified by the production of a large number of offspring with a light investment in the care of each, as employed by reptiles. Humans are situated toward the "K" end of the spectrum, but differentiated by race, such that Africans are the least and Asians the most likely to follow a K strategy, with Europeans falling in between, according to Rushton.[27]

In a series of articles that followed and in his 1995 book, *Race, Evolution, and Behavior*, Rushton expanded upon his K theory.[28] Racial differences, Rushton postulates, arise from the separate evolutionary paths pursued by Africans, Europeans, and Asians, who developed life histories that were shaped by their contrasting environments. A life history is a genetically organized grouping of characteristics, the product of evolution, that allocate energy and employ strategies directed at survival, growth, and reproduction—strategies along the K and r scales. Correlates of those reproductive strategies include brain size, intelligence, maturation speed, development and size of sexual organs, mortality rates, personality, and social phenomena like family formation and stability, ethnocentrism, choice of marriage partners, and even political attitudes.

Asians and Europeans, states Rushton, have the largest brains, but when adjusted for body size, Asians have the largest brains, followed by Europeans, followed by Africans. Greater brain size, according to Rushton, accommodates greater efficiency, which translates into greater intelligence.[29] Most inclined toward a K strategy, Asians exhibit the highest level of sexual inhibition, including a slow rate of maturation and sexual precocity, delayed and low levels of reproductive effort, fewer sexual partners, less frequent sexual intercourse, and less incidence of pregnancy, but these generate greater cultural production and a high degree of social organization. Least inclined toward a K strategy, Africans engage in sexual intercourse earlier, have more sexual partners, have sexual intercourse more frequently, and have a greater incidence of pregnancies. Anatomical differences correspond with those sexual behaviors. Thus, reports Rushton, Asian men have the smallest penises and testes, and Asian women have the smallest vaginas and ovaries, whereas African men have the largest genitalia and African women have the largest vaginas and ovaries, and Asian women begin their menses later than African women, have longer periods, and produce fewer eggs over their fertile lifetimes. Europeans show moderate sexual rates and anatomies, between those of Asians and Africans.[30]

Despite Rushton's proposition that his science, his juxtapositions of "gene-based evolutionary theory with racial differences in sexual behavior," will lead to a greater appreciation of "the nature of human diversity as well as the binding commonalities we share with other species,"[31] his project is saturated with cultural assumptions about the categories of "race" and "racial difference" that emerged from the nineteenth-century need to name and structure natural phenomena and encounters with demonic and benign "others." Rushton is dismissive of his critics' claim that race is a mere social construction, and he disregards his own intuition that "the histories of global populations are genetically complex and linked by intervening gradients,"[32] and thus that racial borders are indistinct and possibly nonexistent. Further, his evidence of measurable and quantifiable differences among and between racialized groups, whether of brain size, intelligence, onset of sexual maturation, reproductive organ size, fre-

quency of sexual intercourse, pregnancy rates, or social categories such as family structures, divorce rates, prejudices, and
political leanings, is at best highly suspect and harkens to an earlier time of biological determinism and eugenics. Instead, Rushton pleads that his theory's alleged predictive value, predictive
of anatomical and behavioral groupings and patterns, renders it
useful and valid.

Rushton's ideas are a return to an earlier time, but they are also
representative of the late twentieth century, despite widespread
rejection of his thesis. Asian men, like their nineteenth-century
stereotype, remain asexual and feminized in Rushton's characterization, and Asian women are less feminine and hence like their
masculinized sisters of the earlier period, but they, in contrast to
their hypersexual reputation of the nineteenth century, are rendered sexually repressed by Rushton. And unlike the previous
century's racial discourse that placed all nonwhites, including
Asians, as the intellectual and cultural inferiors of whites, Rushton's K theory positions Asians above Europeans and Africans in
intelligence and cultural production.[33] At first blush, Rushton
seems to argue for Asian superiority over Africans and, strik-
ingly, over Europeans, reflecting some of his contemporaries' explanations for Asia's post–World War II "economic miracle" and
Asian "success" in assimilating into Canadian and American life.
But when seen in its totality of race, gender, and sexuality, Rushton's representations of both Asians and Africans are as less than
complete individuals and aggregations, the former skewed toward the mind and the latter toward the body. Africans are all
body and no mind—they make good athletes and workers;
Asians are all mind and no body—they are wimps and nerds.
Europeans, situated between those extremes, bear a mediating
genetic architecture that accommodates a diversity of both mind
and body—they are just right. Whatever racial anxiety Asians
might pose because of their alleged intellectual and cultural superiority is mitigated by their bodily inadequacies, which subtext
renders problematic their gender (less "masculine" Asian men,
less "feminine" Asian women) and sexuality (repressed).

As did such representations at the end of the nineteenth century, Rushton's at the end of the twentieth discipline and systematize, but they also install and entrench hierarchies that define privilege and its counterpart, poverty; and they center and empower the originating source—the self—and marginalize and disempower its opposition—the other. The late-nineteenth-century spatial binary of interior and coast, upon which the "new" nationalism was in part built, thus begins with the heartland as an originating and authenticating place of the American spirit, America's soul—the self. By contrast, the coast lies at the exteriors, the extremities, where seemingly alien peoples and influences—the "other"—gain admittance and footholds. That cartography of East and West parallels bodily distinctions of the self's interior as the preserve of purity and its exteriors as sources of pollution. Likewise, the period inventions of self—the West, whiteness, manliness, and heterosexuality—conferred citizenship and community membership and therewith rights and exemptions, whereas largely bereft of those claims were others— the East, nonwhiteness, womanliness, and homosexuality. In truth, the pairs form such oppositions that one is what the other is not, but they also form such correspondences that one requires the other. Further, the binaried geographies, races, genders, and sexualities are linked, one with the other, in a single system of social relations, as in racialized spaces, gendered races, and sexualized genders. They are inseparable.

Binaries, however, refuse multiple or mediating positions that ultimately reveal as illusory the alleged separation and opposition between the social categories and their poles. If there are no fixed, eternal, or universal East and West, nonwhite and white, woman and man, or homosexual and heterosexual, then their powers to designate and bestow freedoms and restrictions are limited. That is why binaries insist upon their unbridgeable gulf—as in East is East and West is West and never the twain shall meet—or try to assimilate into one terminus or the other those positions that disrupt their claim and logic. In 1630, the Virginia governor's council sentenced Hugh Davis, a white man, to a public whipping for "abusing himself to the dishonor of God and shame of Christians by defiling his body in lying with a Negro," in the words of the council. Interracial sex and miscegenation threatened not only white racial "purity," but also the very boundary that ostensibly separated white from nonwhite. The state tried to discourage racial border crossings by classifying the offspring as belonging to the inferior group, such as Virginia's 1787 law that classed as "mulatto" those with one-fourth or more African blood and, more generously in its 1910 law, with one-sixteenth or more, thereby punishing the offenders and their children.[34]

Like "mulattoes," Asians, as neither white nor black, pose a problem for the binary racial border patrol, and have been classed at times as "near-blacks" or "nonwhite" and therewith with their debilities, and at other times as "near-whites" or "model minorities" but without the full natures of whites.[35] And although representations might distinguish and distance oneself from one's other and thereby empower oneself and disempower the other, they might also reveal one's own inadequacies and indeterminacies projected onto the other. The West signifies modernity by relegating the East to tradition. Whites become superior by inventing inferior nonwhites. Men become supermen by creating lesser men and women. Heterosexuals strut by closeting homosexuals. But the West, whites, men, and heterosexuals might be packagings for mixed and dubious contents, and they pose contradictions that, upon reflection, render ambivalent the politics of difference. A stagnant East comforts an energetic West, but it also conditions a crippling self-deception. Inferior Asian racialized bodies elevate racial selves, but also diminish the self's humanity insofar as Asians are human. Feminized Asian men and masculinized Asian women enhance white women's womanliness and white men's manliness, but they also soften the supposed firm definitions and distinctions of "man" and "woman." Highly sexualized Asian women and asexual and homosocial Asian men ensure the normality of white heterosexuality, but they can also whet appetites for perverse pleasures and possibilities. Deviations certify normalcy, but they also prove the elasticity and porousness of the very conventions of geographies, race, gender, and sexuality that are meant to be rigid and impervious, and they can inspire hatreds as well as fire desires.

I have titled this concluding chapter "American History" to underscore the point that history, too, like geographies, race, gender, and sexuality, is an invention. The Asian American subject as represented and asserted, I believe, renders problematic some of the major binaries that sustain the standard renditions of America's past and the hierarchies that constitute its social relations. By foregrounding Asian American history, we come to see that those categories of geographies, race, gender, and sexuality are constructions of the human imagination, that they serve to cohere and reproduce the social order, that they are situated in time and place, and that although fantastic, they are realized and form constraints in our institutions and everyday behaviors. History's texts are likewise implicated and are manufactured by historians, who themselves are products of their places and times and their race, gender, and sexuality.

Consider for a moment the shelves, indeed libraries, of books that bear the title "American History." See them as spatialized, racialized, gendered, and sexualized works—as the products of individuals and their times. America's past, by and large, is conceived of, in those histories, as a place, as a solid, continental space bordered by the westering nation-state. We are made to stand on these shores and watch as immigrants from out there come here to people and settle this land. We are an agrarian people and a European people of a North Atlantic civilization. America thus is a raced place of whites, but also of blacks, who were captured and conveyed in a north and south trans-Atlantic traffic of European manufactures, African labor, and American raw materials. Those formative and monumental activities are the deeds of men, according to those versions of American history, although increasingly we understand them to be the works of both men and women. Usually unstated and assumed are their (hetero)sexualities in normative families and community formations, and in yearnings and couplings deemed natural to child development and maturation. In this, my dissent to those translations of past reality, the Asian American subject asks us to acknowledge those interpretations as craftings that endorse and uphold the hegemony of West over East, white over black, man over woman, and heterosexual over homosexual. And I have offered the Asian American subject as a third position to reconsider those binary oppositions such that, in one sense, there is neither West nor East, white nor black, man nor woman, and heterosexual nor homosexual. But my version, too, is a rendering that was conditioned by my readings of conventional American histories—their subject matters, linear chronologies, and evidentiary sources—and by my intention to contradict and rethink them.

History, accordingly, is at once a script and a performance, a representation and an enactment. Because humans exercise wills and make choices, history is both observed and contested. In truth, even as we make and animate the categories that authorize our lives and histories, we can take them apart and remake and reanimate our selves, our society, and our conceptions of our past to explain anew our present and reimagine our future. I suppose my imperative for including Asians in America's past arises from my understanding of the veracity of that brand of history and from my hope to reconfigure our present and our future—ones that will embrace without reservation both the commonalities and the differences among us. I am sometimes reminded of my peculiarity, my otherness, by selves who fail to distinguish and instead absorb me into their spongy constitutions to render me, apparently, tidy and safe in the assimilation. I am made comprehensible after having been remade in their image. At an event at which I was the featured speaker, I was introduced as the distinguished "Professor Okisaurus," by a father, I presumed, whose child was into dinosaurs, and twice as "Professor Hirohito," by men, perchance, who could at the moment recall only the name of Japan's emperor during World War II. (Both dinosaurs and Japan's wartime emperor are dead! kaput! extinct! I wanted to remind my gracious hosts.) Whatever the reason, I was given a name, a fictional name, like the phony names given to nineteenth-century Chinese women migrants who were uniformly called "Mary."

But I am typical too, a typical American. Despite my name, despite having grown up in Hawaii, my game was cowboys and Indians. But typical is not universal, and my name and my identity are not your name and your identity. There are, in truth, as many American pasts as there are Americans. We are wonderfully heterogeneous. And each of our selves is as complicated and multifaceted as our others. Even as we simultaneously redefine and redeploy our ideas of ourselves as spatialized, racialized, gendered, sexualized, and classed persons within our contexts of history and society, we see and relate to others in a similarly complex way. We do not, indeed cannot, rely upon selves or binaries alone. Either/or is not the entirety. We have numerous other options, thankfully. We do not see ourselves simply as southerners, as Latinas, as men, as lesbians, or as members of the middle class. Likewise, we do not, must not, see geographies configured as either West or East, race as white or black, gender as man or woman, sexuality as heterosexual or homosexual. Constellations abound within each of those systems, and the undulating filaments that connect those supposed oppositions and that lead to other constellations are much too attractive and compelling to ignore. How silly, thus, how monumentally foolish, for any one person or any one group—whether spaced, raced, gendered, sexualized, or classed—to claim the plenitude of America's past, to claim it as singular or to own it as if that person, that group, were the sole purveyors of "American history." The subject, the title, belongs to us all.

But surely choices must be made, limits imposed, and boundaries defined, or else chaos will ensue. "America," after all, is a political entity, a nation-state with borders. "Americans" are its members, and "American history" is its past—indivisible. America, Americans, and American history are all that, to be sure, and more, because our originating source is our multiplicity ("out of many, one" is our motto) and fences are leaped and tunneled under by people, but also by cash, clothes, food, music, and ideas. The frontiers are alive with exchanges and refigurings. Those transactions could involve and lead to controls and exploitations, one over the other, as indeed they have, but they could also map as comely a symmetry and a kinship as we might compose. The choice and the outcome rest with us—we the people. And at the end of this most American of stories, when Dorothy and Toto return home, our dizzying differences, our confounding contradictions, are what we all can agree upon, for it is those that unite us, assemble us as a people, and constitute our common ground.

NOTES

PREFACE

1. Philip J. Deloria, *Playing Indian* (New Haven: Yale University Press, 1998).

2. Gary Y. Okihiro, *Margins and Mainstreams: Asians in American History and Culture* (Seattle: University of Washington Press, 1994).

3. See, e.g., Elizabeth Grosz, *Volatile Bodies: Toward a Corporeal Feminism* (Bloomington: Indiana University Press, 1994).

CHAPTER 1
WEST AND EAST

1. James Thurber, "The Wizard of Chittenango," in *The Wizard of Oz*, edited by Michael Patrick Hearn (New York: Schocken Books, 1983), 160.

2. All are quotes from *The Wonderful Wizard of Oz* are from *The Annotated Wizard of Oz*, edited by Michael Patrick Hearn (New York: Clarkson N. Potter, 1973).

3. Henry M. Littlefield, "The Wizard of Oz: Parable on Populism," in Hearn (ed.), *Wizard of Oz*, 221–33.

4. Brian Attebery, "Oz," in Hearn (ed.), *Wizard of Oz*, 278–304.

5. Frederick Jackson Turner, *The Frontier in American History* (New York: Henry Holt, 1920), 1, 2, 3, 23, 30, 32, 37.

6. Frederick Jackson Turner, "The Significance of History," in *Frontier and Section: Selected Essays of Frederick Jackson Turner*, edited by Ray Allen Billington (Englewood Cliffs, N.J.: Prentice-Hall, 1961), 17, originally published in the *Wisconsin Journal of Education* 21 (October 1891): 230–34 and (November 1891): 253–56.

7. Turner, *The Frontier*, 220–21.

8. Alan Brinkley, *American History: A Survey* (New York: McGraw-Hill, 1995), 511–12; and Cheng-Tsu Wu (ed.), *"Chink!" A Documentary History of Anti-Chinese Prejudice in America* (New York: World Publishing, 1972), 70.

9. Henry Nash Smith, *Virgin Land: The American West as Symbol and Myth* (Cambridge: Harvard University Press, 1950), 4, 11, 260.

10. On the error of that dichotomy, see Joyce Appleby, *Capitalism and a New Social Order: The Republican Vision of the 1790s* (New York: New York University Press, 1984).

11. Smith, *Virgin Land*, 15.

12. Ibid., 21.

13. Ibid., 17, 19.

14. J. Hector St. John de Crèvecoeur, *Letters from an American Farmer* (New York: Fox, Duffield & Co., 1904), 54–55.

15. Henry David Thoreau, "Walking," *Atlantic Monthly,* June 1862.

16. Linda Gordon, *The Great Arizona Orphan Abduction* (Cambridge: Harvard University Press, 1999), 8–13.

17. Walter Havighurst, *The Heartland: Ohio, Indiana, Illinois* (New York: Harper & Row, 1956), 4, 152, 160–61.

18. Martha Mitchell Bigelow, "Michigan: A State in the Vanguard," in *Heartland: Comparative Histories of the Midwestern States,* edited by James H. Madison (Bloomington: Indiana University Press, 1988), 33–34.

19. As cited in Cullom Davis, "Illinois: Crossroads and Cross Section," in Madison, *Heartland,* 130.

20. Howard W. Odum and Harry Estill Moore, *American Regionalism: A Cultural-Historical Approach to National Integration* (New York: Henry Holt, 1938), 462, 463.

21. Carl Becker, "Kansas," in *Essays in American History Dedicated to Frederick Jackson Turner* (New York: Peter Smith, 1951), 88, 107, 110.

22. Ian Tyrrell, "American Exceptionalism in an Age of International History," *American Historical Review* 96, no. 4 (October 1991): 1033.

23. Ibid., 1034–35; and Daniel Bell, " 'American Exceptionalism' Revisited: The Role of Civil Society," *Public Interest* 95 (spring 1989): 41–42.

24. Smith, *Virgin Land,* 6–8, 12.

25. Turner, *The Frontier,* 38.

26. Forrest Davis, *The Atlantic System: The Story of Anglo-American Control of the Seas* (New York: Reynal & Hitchcock, 1941), xi, xii.

27. See, e.g., Ian K. Steele, *The English Atlantic, 1675–1740: An Exploration of Communication and Community* (New York: Oxford University Press, 1986); Marcus Rediker, *Between the Devil and the Deep Blue Sea: Merchant Seamen, Pirates, and the Anglo-American Maritime World, 1700–1750* (Cambridge: Cambridge University Press, 1987); Ralph Davis, *The Rise of Atlantic Economies* (Ithaca: Cornell University Press, 1973); James A. Rawley, *The Transatlantic Slave Trade: A History* (New York: W. W. Norton, 1981); Herbert S. Klein, *African Slavery in Latin America and the Caribbean* (New York: Oxford University Press, 1986); Philip D. Curtin, *The Rise and Fall of the Plantation Complex: Essays in Atlantic History* (Cambridge: Cambridge University Press, 1990); Walter Rodney, *How Europe Underdeveloped Africa* (London: Bogle-L'Ouverture Publications, 1972); Alan L. Karras and J. R. McNeill (eds.), *Atlantic American Societies: From Columbus Through Abolition, 1492–1888* (London: Routledge, 1992); and Paul Gilroy, *The Black Atlantic: Modernity and Double Consiousness* (Cambridge: Harvard University Press, 1993).

28. Gilroy, *Black Atlantic.*

29. For examples of U.S. transnationalist histories, see John Agnew, *The United States in the World-Economy* (New York: Cambridge University Press, 1987); and Randolph Bourne, *History of a Literary Radical* (New York: S. A. Russell, 1956).

30. *The Log of Christopher Columbus*, translated by Robert H. Fuson (Camden, Maine: International Marine Publishing, 1987), 51.

31. *Hippocrates*, translated by W.H.S. Jones (Cambridge: Harvard University Press, 1923), I: 105–33.

32. Edward W. Said, *Orientalism* (New York: Random House, 1978), 1; and Mary B. Campbell, *The Witness and the Other World: Exotic European Travel Writing, 400–1600* (Ithaca: Cornell University Press, 1988), 3. Japan created its own Orientalist discourse in its modernization and imperialism. See Stefan Tanaka, *Japan's Orient: Rendering Pasts into History* (Berkeley: University of California Press, 1993).

33. Said, *Orientalism*, 1, 59, 62, 72, 74, 86, 207–8, 211, 222. For a historicizing of Said's generalizations, see Lisa Lowe, *Critical Terrains: French and British Orientalisms* (Ithaca: Cornell University Press, 1991).

34. Ronald Takaki, *Iron Cages: Race and Culture in 19th-Century America* (New York: Oxford University Press, 1990), 253–79.

35. Cited in Stan Steiner, *Fusang: The Chinese Who Built America* (New York: Harper & Row, 1979), 99–100, 103–5.

36. Smith, *Virgin Land*, 22–29. See also Takaki, *Iron Cages*, 154–56.

37. Smith, *Virgin Land*, 29.

38. For a discussion of the European impact on Asian port cities, see Dilip K. Basu (ed.), *The Rise and Growth of the Colonial Port Cities in Asia* (Santa Cruz: Center for South Pacific Studies, University of California, Santa Cruz, 1979).

39. Marina E. Espina, *Filipinos in Louisiana* (New Orleans, La.: A. F. Laborde & Sons, 1988).

40. Joan M. Jensen, *Passage from India: Asian Indian Immigrants in North America* (New Haven: Yale University Press, 1988), 12–13.

41. John Kuo Wei Tchen, "New York Chinese: The Nineteenth-Century Pre-Chinatown Settlement," *Chinese America: History and Perspectives* (1990): 160–62; and John Kuo Wei Tchen, *New York before Chinatown: Orientalism and the Shaping of American Culture, 1776–1882* (Baltimore: Johns Hopkins University Press, 1999), chap. 4.

42. Jack Chen, *The Chinese of America* (San Francisco: Harper & Row, 1981), 4.

43. Tchen, "New York Chinese," 162, 163.

44. Brinkley, *American History*, 270, 271–72.

45. Jane Addams, *Newer Ideals of Peace* (New York: Macmillan, 1907), 18; and St. Clair Drake and Horace R. Cayton, *Black Metropolis: Study of Negro*

Life in a Northern City, vol. 1 (New York: Harcourt, Brace and Company, 1945), 46–64.

46. See, e.g., Timothy C. Frazer (ed.), *"Heartland" English: Variation and Transition in the American Midwest* (Tuscaloosa: University of Alabama Press, 1993).

47. Vernon Louis Parrington, *Main Currents in American Thought: An Interpretation of American Literature from the Beginnings to 1920* (New York: Harcourt, Brace and Company, 1930), vol. 3, 58.

48. Parrington, *Main Currents,* 58–59. See also John Higham, *Strangers in the Land: Patterns of American Nativism, 1860–1925* (New Brunswick, N.J.: Rutgers University Press, 1963).

49. Robert L. Beisner, *Twelve Against Empire: The Anti-Imperialists, 1898–1900* (New York: McGraw-Hill, 1968), 11.

50. Robert Hunter, *Poverty* (New York: Macmillan, 1904), 261, 262–63, 268.

51. Gary Y. Okihiro, *Margins and Mainstreams: Asians in American History and Culture* (Seattle: University of Washington Press, 1994), 27–28.

52. Nell Irvin Painter, *Standing at Armageddon: The United States, 1877–1919* (New York: W. W. Norton, 1987), 168, 390.

53. As cited in Richard Austin Thompson, *The Yellow Peril, 1890–1924* (New York: Arno Press, 1978), 4, 18–21.

54. For the late twentieth century, see Juan F. Perea (ed.), *Immigrants Out! The New Nativism and the Anti-Immigrant Impulse in the United States* (New York: New York University Press, 1997).

CHAPTER 2
WHITE AND BLACK

1. Michael Patrick Hearn, *The Annotated Wizard of Oz* (New York: Clarkson N. Potter, 1973), 201.

2. Donald L. Miller, *City of the Century: The Epic of Chicago and the Making of America* (New York: Simon & Schuster, 1996), 488, 491.

3. Ibid., 491–92, 495, 496.

4. John J. Flinn (comp.), *Official Guide to the World's Columbian Exposition* (Chicago: John Anderson, 1893), 7, 9.

5. Robert W. Rydell, *All the World's a Fair: Visions of Empire at American International Expositions, 1876–1916* (Chicago: University of Chicago Press, 1984), 48–52.

6. Anonymous, *The Columbian Gallery: A Portfolio of Photographs from the World's Fair* (Chicago: Werner Company, 1894), 1.

7. William E. Cameron et al., *The World's Fair, Being a Pictorial History of the Columbian Exposition* (Syracuse, N.Y.: H. C. Leavenworth, 1893), 642.

8. Ben[jamin] C. Truman, *History of the World's Fair Being a Complete and Authentic Description of the Columbian Exposition from Its Inception* (Philadelphia: Mammoth Publishing, 1893), 549, 550.

9. *Columbian Gallery*, 1.

10. *Columbian Gallery*, 3; and Cameron, *World's Fair*, 674.

11. *Columbian Gallery*, 4. See also David F. Burg, *Chicago's White City of 1893* (Lexington: University Press of Kentucky, 1976), 222.

12. *Columbian Gallery*, 4; and Cameron, *World's Fair*, 674.

13. Rydell, *All the World's a Fair*, 52; and Elliott M. Rudwick and August Meier, "Black Man in the 'White City': Negroes and the Columbian Exposition, 1893," *Phylon* 26, no. 4 (winter 1965): 356, 359.

14. Truman, *History of the World's Fair*, 588.

15. Rydell, *All the World's a Fair*, 55, 57.

16. L. G. Moses, "Indians on the Midway: Wild West Shows and the Indian Bureau at World's Fairs, 1893–1904," *South Dakota History* 21, no. 3 (fall 1991): 210–14; and L. G. Moses, *Wild West Shows and the Images of American Indians, 1883–1933* (Albuquerque: University of New Mexico Press, 1996), chap. 7.

17. Rydell, *All the World's a Fair*, 65, 66.

18. Anonymous, *The Dream City: A Portfolio of Photographic Views of the World's Columbian Exposition* (St. Louis, Mo.: N. D. Thompson, 1893); and Truman, *History of the World's Fair*, 567, 568.

19. *Columbian Gallery*, 7–9; and Truman, *History of the World's Fair*, 571–73.

20. Alan Trachtenberg, *The Incorporation of America: Culture and Society in the Gilded Age* (New York: Hill and Wang, 1982), 209, 211–13. See also William Cronon, *Nature's Metropolis: Chicago and the Great West* (New York: W. W. Norton, 1991), 342.

21. Reginald Horsman, *Race and Manifest Destiny: The Origins of American Racial Anglo-Saxonism* (Cambridge: Harvard University Press, 1981), 98–115.

22. Quoted in Richard Drinnon, *Facing West: The Metaphysics of Indian-Hating and Empire-Building* (New York: New American Library, 1980), 65.

23. George M. Fredrickson, *The Black Image in the White Mind: The Debate on Afro-American Character and Destiny, 1817–1914* (New York: Harper & Row, 1971), 134, 135.

24. Ibid., 144–45.

25. Thomas F. Gossett, *Race: The History of an Idea in America* (Dallas, Tex.: Southern Methodist University Press, 1963), 262.

26. Fredrickson, *Black Image*, 245, 246, 248.

27. Josiah Strong, *Our Country: Its Possible Future and Its Present Crisis* (New York: Baker & Taylor, 1885), 159, 160, 161, 175.

28. Ibid., 170, 171.

29. Horsman, *Race and Manifest Destiny*, 9–24.

30. David R. Roediger, *The Wages of Whiteness: Race and the Making of the American Working Class* (London: Verso, 1991), 133–34.

31. Ibid., 140–50.

32. Horsman, *Race and Manifest Destiny,* 253.

33. Ibid., 252.

34. See, e.g., Bill Ong Hing, *Making and Remaking Asian America Through Immigration Policy, 1850–1990* (Stanford: Stanford University Press, 1993).

35. Sucheng Chan, "The Exclusion of Chinese Women, 1870–1943," in *Entry Denied: Exclusion and the Chinese Community in America, 1882–1943,* edited by Sucheng Chan (Philadelphia: Temple University Press, 1991), 105–9.

36. Quoted in Lucy E. Salyer, *Laws Harsh as Tigers: Chinese Immigrants and the Shaping of Modern Immigration Law* (Chapel Hill: University of North Carolina Press, 1995), 15.

37. See John W. Cell, *The Highest Stage of White Supremacy: The Origins of Segregation in South Africa and the American South* (Cambridge: Cambridge University Press, 1982).

38. Alexander Saxton, *The Indispensable Enemy: Labor and the Anti-Chinese Movement in California* (Berkeley: University of California Press, 1971), 19.

39. Quoted in Alexander Saxton, *The Rise and Fall of the White Republic: Class Politics and Mass Culture in Nineteenth-Century America* (London: Verso, 1990), 296.

40. Fredrickson, *Black Image,* 266. Cf. John Higham, *Strangers in the Land: Patterns of American Nativism, 1860–1925* (New Brunswick, N.J.: Rutgers University Press, 1955), 165–67. Higham sees regional disjunctions and distinguishes among nativisms directed against African Americans and European, Chinese, and Japanese immigrants.

41. Graham Hodges, " 'Desirable Companions and Lovers': Irish and African Americans in the Sixth Ward, 1830–1870," in *The New York Irish,* edited by Ronald H. Bayor and Timothy J. Meagher (Baltimore: Johns Hopkins University Press, 1996), 107–24. See also Roediger, *Wages of Whiteness,* 144–56.

42. John Kuo Wei Tchen, "Quimbo Appo's Fear of Fenians: Chinese-Irish-Anglo Relations in New York City," in Bayor and Meagher (eds.), *New York Irish,* 125–52. Chinese men (as well as Asian Indians) often took on Anglo names; John Huston was Chinese.

43. James Baldwin, "On Being 'White' . . . And Other Lies," *Essence* 14, no. 12 (April 1984): 90.

44. Charles J. McClain, *In Search of Equality: The Chinese Struggle against Discrimination in Nineteenth-Century America* (Berkeley: University of California Press, 1994), 20–22; Okihiro, *Margins and Mainstreams,* 50–51; and Wu, "*Chink!,*" 36–43.

45. McClain, *In Search of Equality,* 71–73; Salyer, *Laws Harsh as Tigers,* 13; and Ian F. Haney Lopez, *White by Law: The Legal Construction of Race* (New York: New York University Press, 1996), 54–55.

46. Haney Lopez, *White by Law*, 61, 67, 203–7.

47. Ibid., 86–92; and Jensen, *Passage from India*, 264.

48. Karen Isaksen Leonard, *Making Ethnic Choices: California's Punjabi Mexican Americans* (Philadelphia: Temple University Press, 1992), 68.

49. Haney Lopez, *White by Law*, 118–19. See also F. James Davis, *Who Is Black? One Nation's Definition* (University Park: Pennsylvania State University Press, 1991).

50. Tomas Almaguer, *Racial Fault Lines: The Historical Origins of White Supremacy in California* (Berkeley: University of California Press, 1994), 45–74.

51. Lucy M. Cohen, *Chinese in the Post–Civil War South: A People without a History* (Baton Rouge: Louisiana State University Press, 1984), 167–68.

52. Quoted in McClain, *In Search of Equality*, 22.

53. Haney Lopez, *White by Law*, 148–49.

54. Kelly Miller, *The Everlasting Stain* (Washington, D.C.: Associated Publishers, 1924), 163.

55. "Some Reasons for Chinese Exclusion. Meat vs. Rice. American Manhood against Asiatic Coolieism," 57th Congress, 1st sess., Senate, Document no. 137 (Washington, D.C.: Government Printing Office, 1902), 24.

56. See Lisa Lowe, *Immigrant Acts: On Asian American Cultural Politics* (Durham, N.C.: Duke University Press, 1996), 1–36.

57. Quoted in Haney Lopez, *White by Law*, 55–56.

CHAPTER 3
MAN AND WOMAN

1. Quoted in Robert W. Rydell, *All the World's a Fair: Visions of Empire at American International Expositions, 1876–1916* (Chicago: University of Chicago Press, 1984), 67.

2. John J. Flinn (comp.), *Official Guide to the World's Columbian Exposition* (Chicago: John Anderson, 1893), 121–22.

3. Department of Publicity and Promotion (ed.), *World's Columbian Exposition, 1893: Official Catalogue*, Part 14, Woman's Building (Chicago: W. B. Conkey, 1893), 62; Ben[jamin] C. Truman, *History of the World's Fair Being a Complete and Authentic Description of the Columbian Exposition from Its Inception* (Philadelphia: Mammoth Publishing, 1893), 165–66, 187–92; and Flinn, *Official Guide*, 121–28.

4. Rydell, *All the World's a Fair*, 59–60.

5. David F. Burg, *Chicago's White City of 1893* (Lexington: University Press of Kentucky, 1976), 164–66.

6. Donald L. Miller, *City of the Century: The Epic of Chicago and the Making of America* (New York: Simon & Schuster, 1996), 504.

7. Truman, *History of the World's Fair*, 187, 188, 189.

8. Ibid., 163–64, 165.

9. Flinn, *Official Guide*, 121, 123.

10. Quoted in Truman, *History of the World's Fair*, 175–83.

11. Miller, *City of the Century*, 502.

12. Burg, *Chicago's White City*, 106.

13. Gail Bederman, *Manliness & Civilization: A Cultural History of Gender and Race in the United States, 1880–1917* (Chicago: University of Chicago Press, 1995), 34.

14. Burg, *Chicago's White City*, 143–44.

15. Edward H. Clarke, *Sex in Education; or, A Fair Chance for the Girls* (1873; reprint, New York: Arno Press, 1972), 102–4, 112–17.

16. Elizabeth Stuart Phelps, in *Sex and Education: A Reply to Dr. E. H. Clarke's "Sex in Education,"* edited by Julia Ward Howe (Boston: Roberts Brothers, 1874), 126–38. (Reprint, New York: Arno Press, 1972), 130–36. I am grateful to my colleague Sarah Deutsch for calling my attention to these documents.

17. Quoted in Truman, *History of the World's Fair*, 179.

18. Truman, *History of the World's Fair*, 179.

19. Mary P. Ryan, *Womanhood in America: From Colonial Times to the Present* (New York: New Viewpoints, 1979), 75–150.

20. Bederman, *Manliness & Civilization*, 15.

21. Anonymous, *The Dream City; The Vanished City: The World's Columbian Exposition in Pen and Picture* (Chicago: Werner Company, n.d.); Rydell, *All the World's a Fair*, 66; Truman, *History of the World's Fair*, 565–73; and Bederman, *Manliness & Civilization*, 35–41.

22. Fredrickson, *Black Image*, 101, 105, 106, 110–11,

23. As quoted in Horsman, *Race and Manifest Destiny*, 233.

24. Ibid., 234.

25. Quoted in Bederman, *Manliness & Civilization*, 175.

26. Russell Roth, *Muddy Glory: America's 'Indian Wars' in the Philippines* (West Hanover, Mass.: Christopher Publishing, 1981), 24.

27. Alexander Saxton, *The Rise and Fall of the White Republic: Class Politics and Mass Culture in Nineteenth-Century America* (London: Verso, 1990), 370, 371, 373, 375; and Bederman, *Manliness & Civilization*, 170–215.

28. *Rudyard Kipling's Verse, 1885–1926* (Garden City, N.Y.: Doubleday, Page & Company, 1927), 373–74.

29. Peggy Pascoe, "Gender Systems in Conflict: The Marriages of Mission-Educated Chinese American Women, 1874–1939," *Journal of Social History* 22, no. 4 (summer 1989): 634, 636–37.

30. Irving Wallace and Amy Wallace, *The Two: A Biography* (New York: Simon and Schuster, 1978), 35, 47–48, 52, 55, 129, 135, 162, 177–79, 187–91, 222. For a recent discussion of Chinese "curiosities," see Tchen, *New York*

before Chinatown, chap. 5; and Robert G. Lee, *Orientals: Asian Americans in Popular Culture* (Philadelphia: Temple University Press, 1999), 28–33.

31. John Kuo Wei Tchen, "New York Chinese: The Nineteenth-Century Pre-Chinatown Settlement," *Chinese America: History and Perspectives* (1990): 158–59; and Wallace and Wallace, *The Two*, 225.

32. Miller, *City of the Century*, 504.

33. Wallace and Wallace, *The Two*, 173, 175.

34. Ibid., 175, 187–91.

35. Quoted in Thomas W. Chinn (ed.), *A History of the Chinese in California: A Syllabus* (San Francisco: Chinese Historical Society of America, 1969), 64.

36. Robert Louis Stevenson, *Across the Plains, with Other Memories and Essays* (New York: Charles Scribner's Sons, 1900), 62, 65–66.

37. Jay Geller, "Judenzopf/Chinesenzopf: Of Jews and Queues," *Positions* 2, no. 3 (winter 1994): 500–37.

38. Pierre Loti, "Japanese Women," *Harper's Monthly* 82 (December 1890): 119, 120, 124, 126, 130, 131. I am grateful to my former student, Amy L. Blair, for pointing this out to me.

39. Quoted from Loti's book *Japoneries d'Automne* in *Once Upon a Time: Visions of Old Japan* (originally published in France as *Mukashi, Mukashi, 1863–1883*), translated by Linda Coverdale (New York: Friendly Press, 1986), 26–27.

40. Quoted in Richard Saunders, *Ambrose Bierce: The Making of a Misanthrope* (San Francisco: Chronicle Books, 1985), 15.

41. Ambrose Bierce, "The Haunted Valley," *Overland Monthly* 7, no. 1 (July 1871): 88–95.

42. For another reading of Bierce's "Haunted Valley," see Lee, *Orientals*, 91–97.

43. "Some Reasons for Chinese Exclusion. Meat vs. Rice."

44. Lee Chew, "The Biography of a Chinaman," *Independent* 55 (February 19, 1903): 417–23.

45. Quoted in Bederman, *Manliness & Civilization*, 36.

CHAPTER 4
HETEROSEXUAL AND HOMOSEXUAL

1. *Columbian Gallery: A Portfolio of Photographs from the World's Fair* (Chicago: Werner Company, 1894), 4, 5, 6.

2. John D'Emilio and Estelle B. Freedman, *Intimate Matters: A History of Sexuality in America* (New York: Harper & Row, 1988), 85–86, 95, 96.

3. Deborah Gray White, *Ar'n't I a Woman? Female Slaves in the Plantation South* (New York: W. W. Norton, 1985), 30, 32–33, 35–38, 39–43, 44–45, 46, 49. On sexual standards among slave women, see Herbert G. Gutman,

"Marital and Sexual Norms Among Slave Women," in *A Heritage of Her Own: Toward a New Social History of American Women*, edited by Nancy F. Cott and Elizabeth H. Pleck (New York: Simon and Schuster, 1979), 298–310.

4. D'Emilio and Freedman, *Intimate Matters*, 87, 88, 91–92, 93. See also Richard C. Trexler, *Sex and Conquest: Gendered Violence, Political Order, and the European Conquest of the Americas* (Ithaca: Cornell University Press, 1995).

5. D'Emilio and Freedman, *Intimate Matters*, 90; and Glenda Riley, *Women and Indians on the Frontier, 1825–1915* (Albuquerque: University of New Mexico Press, 1984), 181.

6. Riley, *Women and Indians*, 122, 123, 129.

7. Evelyn Blackwood, "Sexuality and Gender in Certain Native American Tribes: The Case of Cross-Gender Females," in *Theorizing Feminism: Parallel Trends in the Humanities and Social Sciences*, edited by Anne C. Herrman and Abigail J. Stewart (Boulder, Colo.: Westview Press, 1994), 302, 310. See also Harriet Whitehead, "The Bow and the Burden Strap: A New Look at Institutionalized Homosexuality in Native North America," in *Sexual Meanings: The Cultural Construction of Gender and Sexuality*, edited by Sherry B. Ortner and Harriet Whitehead (Cambridge: Cambridge University Press, 1981), 80–115, for a review of the ethnographic literature on American Indian gender and sexual inversions.

8. Quoted in George Chauncey Jr., "From Sexual Inversion to Homosexuality: Medicine and the Changing Conception of Female Deviance," *Salmagundi* 58–59 (fall 1982/winter 1983): 119. For a complex rendering of Victorian "passionless" women, see Nancy F. Cott, "Passionless: An Interpretation of Victorian Sexual Ideology, 1790–1850," in Cott and Pleck, *A Heritage of Her Own*, 162–81.

9. Chauncey, "From Sexual Inversion to Homosexuality," 116–17.

10. Jeffrey Weeks, *Sexuality* (Chichester, England: Ellis Horwood, 1986), 45.

11. Kevin J. Mumford, "Homosex Changes: Race, Cultural Geography, and the Emergence of the Gay," *American Quarterly* 48, no. 3 (September 1996), 399.

12. Peggy Pascoe, "Miscegenation Law, Court Cases, and Ideologies of 'Race' in Twentieth-Century America," *Journal of American History* 83, no. 1 (June 1996): 48, fn. 11; and Mumford, "Homosex Changes," 399.

13. Hugh A. Tinker, *A New System of Slavery: The Export of Indian Labour Overseas, 1830–1920* (London: Oxford University Press, 1974); and Robert J. Schwendinger, *Ocean of Bitter Dreams: Maritime Relations Between China and the United States, 1850–1915* (Tucson, Ariz.: Westernlore Press, 1988).

14. M.G.C. Edholm, "A Stain on the Flag," *Californian Illustrated Magazine* 1 (February 1892): 162, 163–65.

15. O. Gibson, *The Chinese in America* (Cincinnati, Ohio: Hitchcock & Walden, 1877), 139.

16. Lucie Cheng, "Free, Indentured, Enslaved: Chinese Prostitutes in Nineteenth-Century America," in *Labor Immigration Under Capitalism: Asian Workers in the United States Before World War II*, edited by Lucie Cheng and Edna Bonacich (Berkeley: University of California Press, 1984), 408–9.

17. Curt Gentry, *The Madams of San Francisco: An Irreverent History of the City by the Golden Gate* (Garden City, N.Y.: Doubleday, 1964), 51, 52.

18. Stephen Longstreet (ed.), *Nell Kimball: Her Life as an American Madam by Herself* (New York: Macmillan, 1970), 227.

19. Quoted in Yong Chen, "China in America: A Cultural Study of Chinese San Francisco, 1850–1943," Ph.D. dissertation, Cornell University, 1993, 57, 59.

20. Longstreet, *Nell Kimball*, 228.

21. Ibid., 227, 228.

22. Mary Roberts Coolidge, *Chinese Immigration* (New York: Henry Holt and Company, 1909), 23, 24, 401, 455.

23. Edholm, "Stain on the Flag," 159, 165, 169, 170. See also Laurene Wu McClain, "Donaldina Cameron: A Reappraisal," *Pacific Historian* 27, no. 3 (fall 1983): 25–35.

24. Charles E. Rosenberg, "Sexuality, Class and Role in 19th-Century America," *American Quarterly* 25, no. 2 (May 1973): 143, 144.

25. Cited in Elmer Clarence Sandmeyer, *The Anti-Chinese Movement in California* (Urbana: University of Illinois Press, 1973), 25.

26. See, e.g., Chris Friday, *Organizing Asian American Labor: The Pacific Coast Canned-Salmon Industry, 1870–1942* (Philadelphia: Temple University Press, 1994), 54–55. On Asian, African American, and white male prostitutes and Asian American men, see H. Brett Melendy, *Asians in America: Filipinos, Koreans, and East Indians* (New York: Hippocrene Books, 1981), 82; and Jack Masson and Donald Guimary, "Asian Labor Contractors in the Alaskan Canned Salmon Industry: 1880–1937," *Labor History* 22, no. 3 (summer 1981): 391.

27. Clifford P. Westermeier, "The Cowboy and Sex," in *The Cowboy: Six-Shooters, Songs, and Sex*, edited by Charles W. Harris and Buck Rainey (Norman: University of Oklahoma Press, 1976), 95–97.

28. Gary Y. Okihiro, *Margins and Mainstreams: Asians in American History and Culture* (Seattle: University of Washington Press, 1994), 118–19.

29. Quoted in Roger Daniels, *The Politics of Prejudice: The Anti-Japanese Movement in California and the Struggle for Japanese Exclusion* (New York: Atheneum, 1970), 20, 47.

30. Ibid., 85; and Dennis M. Ogawa, *From Japs to Japanese: The Evolution of Japanese-American Stereotypes* (Berkeley, Calif.: McCutchan Publishing, 1971), 15.

31. Roger Daniels, *Concentration Camps: North America* (Malabar, Fla.: Robert E. Krieger Publishing, 1981), 15.

32. Gina Marchetti, *Romance and the "Yellow Peril": Race, Sex, and Discursive Strategies in Hollywood Fiction* (Berkeley: University of California Press, 1993), 14.

33. H. A. Millis, *The Japanese Problem in the United States* (New York: Macmillan, 1915), 247.

34. H. Brett Melendy, "Filipinos in the United States," in *The Asian American: The Historical Experience,* edited by Norris Hundley Jr. (Santa Barbara: Clio Books, 1976), 123.

35. C. M. Goethe, "Filipino Immigration Viewed as a Peril," *Current History* (June 1931): 354.

36. Daniel J. Kevles, *In the Name of Eugenics: Genetics and the Uses of Human Heredity* (New York: Alfred A. Knopf, 1985), 107.

37. For example, see the following studies on culture and personality from the 1950s and 1960s that contrast the normative heterosexualities of white men and women with the repressed heterosexualities of Chinese and Japanese American men and women. Abe Arkoff, "Need Patterns in Two Generations of Japanese Americans in Hawaii," *Journal of Social Psychology* 50 (1959): 75–79; and Walter D. Fenz and Abe Arkoff, "Comparative Need Patterns of Five Ancestry Groups in Hawaii," *Journal of Social Psychology* 58 (1962): 67–89.

38. Bruno Lasker, *Filipino Immigration to Continental United States and to Hawaii* (Chicago: University of Chicago Press, 1931), 98; and Melendy, "Filipinos in the United States," 120.

39. Eugene Franklin Wong, *On Visual Media Racism: Asians in the American Motion Pictures* (New York: Arno Press, 1978), 74.

40. Cited in Robert A. Padgug, "Sexual Matters: On Conceptualizing Sexuality in History," *Radical History Review* 20 (spring/summer 1979): 9.

41. D'Emilio and Freedman, *Intimate Matters,* 86.

CHAPTER 5
AMERICAN HISTORY

1. As reported by Joyce Wadler, "The Spy Who Fell in Love with a Shadow," *New York Times Magazine,* August 15, 1993, 54.

2. This account is taken from Wadler, "The Spy," 30–32, 36–38, 48, 50, 53–54.

3. Ibid., 53.

4. Ibid., 54.

5. Giacomo Puccini, *Seven Puccini Librettos,* translated by William Weaver (New York: W. W. Norton, 1981).

6. David Henry Hwang, *M. Butterfly* (New York: Penguin Books, 1986), 94, 95.

7. Ibid., 1, 2.

8. Dorinne K. Kondo, "*M. Butterfly*: Orientalism, Gender, and a Critique of Essentialist Identity," *Cultural Critique* 16 (fall 1990): 15; and Dorinne K. Kondo, *About Face: Performing Race in Fashion and Theater* (New York: Routledge, 1997), 31–54.

9. Hwang, *M. Butterfly*, 90, 91, 92.

10. Ibid., 17.

11. Ibid., 88, 89.

12. Ibid., 93.

13. John Gawsworth (comp.), *The Best Stories of Thomas Burke* (London: Phoenix House, 1950), 8.

14. Ibid., 12.

15. See Lisa Lowe, *Critical Terrains: French and British Orientalisms* (Ithaca: Cornell University Press, 1991).

16. Thomas Burke, *Limehouse Nights* (London: Grosset & Dunlap, 1917), 15, 21.

17. On boxing and manliness, see Elliott J. Gorn, *The Manly Art: Bare-Knuckle Prize Fighting in America* (Ithaca: Cornell University Press, 1986), especially its prologue.

18. Ibid., 15, 16, 17, 18, 19, 21.

19. On Victorian constructions of the child and sexuality, see James R. Kinkaid, *Child-Loving: The Erotic Child and Victorian Culture* (New York: Routledge, 1992).

20. Burke, *Limehouse Nights*, 18,

21. Ibid., 23, 24, 26, 27, 28, 29, 30.

22. Ibid., 22, 23.

23. Ibid., 31–37.

24. Ludmilla Jordanova, *Sexual Visions: Images of Gender in Science and Medicine between the Eighteenth and Twentieth Centuries* (Madison: University of Wisconsin Press, 1989), 22, 23.

25. See, e.g., James Davison Hunter, *Culture Wars: The Struggle to Define America* (New York: Basic Books, 1990); Samuel P. Huntington, *The Clash of Civilizations and the Remaking of World Order* (New York: Simon and Schuster, 1996); Peter Brimelow, *Alien Nation: Common Sense about America's Immigration Disaster* (New York: Random House, 1995); George Friedman and Meredith Lebard, *The Coming War With Japan* (New York: St. Martin's Press, 1991); and Richard Bernstein and Ross H. Munro, *The Coming Conflict With China* (New York: Alfred A. Knopf, 1997).

26. Quotes from Ronald Takaki, *Strangers from a Different Shore: A History of Asian Americans* (Boston: Little, Brown, 1989), 481–84. See also U.S. Com-

mission on Civil Rights, *Civil Rights Issues Facing Asian Americans in the 1990s* (Washington, D.C., 1992), 25–26.

27. J. Philippe Rushton, "Differential K Theory: The Sociobiology of Individual and Group Differences," *Personality and Individual Differences* 6, no. 4 (1985): 441–52.

28. J. Philippe Rushton, "Differential K Theory and Race Differences in E and N," *Personality and Individual Differences* 6, no. 6 (1985): 769–70; J. Philippe Rushton and Anthony F. Bogaert, "Race Differences in Sexual Behavior: Testing an Evolutionary Hypothesis," *Journal of Research in Personality* 21, no. 4 (December 1987): 529–51; J. Philippe Rushton and Anthony F. Bogaert, "Race versus Social Class Differences in Sexual Behavior: A Follow-up Test of the r/K Dimension," *Journal of Research in Personality* 22, no. 3 (September 1988): 259–72; and J. Philippe Rushton, *Race, Evolution, and Behavior: A Life History Perspective* (New Brunswick, N.J.: Transaction, 1995).

29. Rushton, *Race, Evolution, and Behavior*, 113–46.

30. Rushton and Bogaert, "Race Differences in Sexual Behavior"; and Rushton, *Race, Evolution, and Behavior*, 165–83.

31. Rushton and Bogaert, "Race Differences in Sexual Behavior," 547.

32. Rushton, *Race, Evolution, and Behavior*, 235.

33. For another recent discussion of race, class, and intelligence and the alleged intellectual superiority of East Asians, see, Richard J. Herrnstein and Charles Murray, *The Bell Curve: Intelligence and Class Structure in American Life* (New York: Free Press, 1994).

34. Philip R. Reilly, *The Surgical Solution: A History of Involuntary Sterilization in the United States* (Baltimore: Johns Hopkins University Press, 1991), 72.

35. See, e.g., Okihiro, *Margins and Mainstreams*, 31–63, 118–47.